NOT FOR THIS
LIFE ONLY

REVISED EDITION

A Study for Growth Into Maturity as a
Child of God - for today and for eternity.

IRVIN STAPF

BOOKSIDE Press

BookSide Press
877-741-8091
www.booksidepress.com
orders@booksidepress.com

DEDICATION

To My Wife, Audrey

Our Gracious Lord brought us together fifty seven years ago, allowing us to share His image and grow together in His love.

For Audrey's love, service, and dedication to me and to our Lord Jesus Christ, this book is dedicated to her. My love for her and the family she has given me, is second only to my love for our Lord.

Introduction

In the process of looking for something on Google, I ran across a blog that caught my attention. It was from J.D. and posed the question "Is there an overarching and knowable purpose to our existence?" Wow! That is a broad question and the one I seek to address in the following chapters. J.D., however, answers it in quite a different manner than I do. J.D. said,

> "I don't have religion, but I do believe there is some purpose, or multiple purposes to life. I don't believe there are any external purposes to life. Any purpose to an individual life must come from inside. Since I do not believe in the existence of a god, I believe that any purpose that you find from your belief and worship is actually coming from inside and not from a Creator. This does not make the purpose any less valid in my eyes. So how does one derive a purpose in life if there is no god? It is my opinion that this internal motivation is entirely personal. Each will have his own purpose. Ultimately, the same general goal is at stake, though - individual happiness."

J. D. goes on for another page and a half, but the thrust of his argument is here. JD says "the same general goal" is at stake for all people. He identifies this as "individual happiness".

This is not unique with J.D. The same thoughts in much more developed form were voiced by Thomas Hobbes in the 17th century, and Jeremy Benthan in the 18th. Benthan following Hobbes concluded "that the greatest happiness of the greatest number will be (achieved) when each individual does all in his power to achieve his personal maximum of genuine and enduring happiness."[1] Hobbes at least recognized that man is by nature a selfish animal constantly in conflict with his fellows.

From Holy Scripture we understand this as our corrupt nature from the Fall, from our first rebellion from God's command.

Similar thoughts were embodied in the Enlightenment and the French Revolution by the cry of "liberty, equality, fraternity." It is in our own Declaration of Independence as our "right to life, liberty, and the pursuit of happiness." But without some absolute values, some unchanging purpose beyond the individual, these high sounding goals are never reached. Happiness is not the lot of the majority of the world's people, and it is not even within the reach of many regardless of the choices they make. Further, without an external absolute will, moral values cease to exist, and without this, civilization ceases to exist. Peter Kreeft, analyzing C. S. Lewis' *The Abolition of Man* says, "We are the first civilization that does not know why we exist. Every past civilization has had some religious answer to that question. The essence of modernity is the abandoning of that religious foundation, ..." [2] (Just as J.D. has.) "So there is no morality without moral absolutes. But there can be no moral absolutes without God. An absolute law can come from and be enforced only by an absolute will. Finally, no civilization can stand without morality."

Individual Happiness

Actually, our Lord would not disagree that individual happiness is the desire of all people and His desire for us. The Bible begins with the account in Genesis of the Lord God creating mankind in a garden paradise without sin. Even after our rebellion God promised a Redeemer that would provide the path to redemption and restoration. After many years of trials and pain God never abandon His creation. Speaking through the Prophet Jeremiah He said, "For I know the plans I have for you," declares the LORD, "plans to prosper you and not to harm you, plans to give you hope and a future." (Jeremiah 29:11) In the New Testament Jesus speaks about God's Kingdom comparing it to a great wedding banquet.

Even the kind of individual happiness that JD envisions can't compare with the future our Lord desires for each of us.

But JD gives himself and mankind far too much credit for the ability to achieve happiness apart from God, and apart from the moral foundation that only He can provide. JD identified the fault in his own reasoning, but is unwilling to acknowledge it. He says that the only condition is that "one person's happiness must not infringe upon another's". Ah! There's the problem! What is inside of us invariably will "infringe upon another's". Every daily new report displays this in banner headlines. What comes from inside multi-millions of individuals setting their own direction can only lead to chaos and ultimately death.

My wife and I still get a daily newspaper. I usually read the comics page first. It invariably shows us images of mankind's true nature. Occasionally though it also provides some good theological truth. *Pearls before Swine* is a regular cartoon strip drawn by Stephen Pastis. On a recent Sunday Pastis drew one of his central characters, Rat, viewing a TV program that declared, "The Key, really, is to just encourage people to be themselves." Further cartoon panels emphasizing the same thing. Even a Spiritual Retreat banner advertising 'Learning to Be Yourself'. Finally Rat screams "The problem in the world is not that people aren't being themselves! It's that they ARE being themselves!" Very true! People are being themselves and acting out of their own fallen nature.

In our Lutheran worship service we begin each week acknowledging both our corrupt nature and hearing the declaration of our forgiveness and redemption in Jesus Christ. This is not of ourselves it is a gift of God's grace. It is the only true foundation upon which we can build our lives and come to the happiness we and our Lord desires.

Individual *happiness is desired for all people*. For that to be true for all there must be *moral absolutes* that are common for all. And for there to be common moral absolutes there must be *a single will of the Creator God.*

Many Earthly Pursuits But One Way

For many years I was what is generally called a worker priest. That is I served my congregation as their pastor, but I also earned part of our family's income in a secular trade. I was a woodworker operating my own shop for 30 years. I made furniture, cabinetry, signs, and generally anything small or large as requested. I learned a great deal about our God, strange as it may seem, even through woodworking methods.

I had to make decisions about how accomplish my end product. Often there were not many possible ways to do the task but only one. The picture of that one finished result remained in my mind through all the necessary stages. Some required cutting; some carving; some separating the good from the bad; some required precise measurements in order to join one piece into another. You get the picture. You've likely done the same whether working to repair a car, or baking a cake.

We've all seen the news reports in our space exploration age about the successes and failures of landing a craft on the moon. This is an incredibly complex program and requires hundreds of highly trained people to accomplish. Even one small deviation can cause the failure of the entire project. And there have been more failures than successes, even though it is the successful missions that we acknowledge and applaud.

Each individual human being, both physically and mentally, is the most complex structure ever assembled. If we add to this all of the other parts of the animal and vegetable world, each having their own individual structure, the complexity is beyond the grasp of anyone. Yet even in our broken world we do see places where order and harmony functions. There is a unique design to establish order for each part of the physical universe God created. He, in fact, is the master Potter, and we are the clay.

Our goal, the finished product of our life, is not from within us but very much established by our Creator. "Know that the Lord Himself is God; It is He who has made us, and not we ourselves; We are His people and the sheep of His pasture." (Psalm 100:3) This is not the time that we enter a debate of Creation vs. evolution. I leave that for others, though I strongly confess and base this text on the truth of our Creator God. And since God is our Creator it is He who established the only way it can be accomplished for all people. Without standards, common values, laws held by all, individual goals, desires, and paths to individual happiness will always conflict with one another.

Train up a child

Solomon the son of David, king of Israel, is credited with giving us the book of Proverbs. "To know wisdom and instruction,
To discern the sayings of understanding,
To receive instruction in wise behavior,
Righteousness, justice and equity;
To give prudence to the simple ones,
To the youth knowledge and discretion,
A wise man will hear and increase in learning,
And a man of understanding will acquire wise counsel,
The words of the wise and their riddles.
The fear of the Lord is the beginning of knowledge;
Fools despise wisdom and instruction."
(Proverbs 1:1-7)

Moving down to the 6th verse of chapter 22 we are instructed to "Train up a child in the way he should go and when he is old he will not depart from it."

When a child comes into the life of a family, parents want the best for that child. We want it for all of our children and are willing to spend many hours and a substantial part of our income for the children's growth and well being. It is a parents joy to watch their children grow, learn, and achieve new heights.

They may follow their parents vocational fields, or strike out on something completely different. Either way the parents can rejoice in their offspring's accomplishments. What then is the common factor that the Proverb author is speaking about in "the way" a child should be trained? That is what this book is about. Training for life. But let's be clear about these two words.

In the mind of the proverb writer training had a single over arching focus that he calls "the way". It has been outlined in those first 7 verses of Chapter 1. He is referring to a set of values, standards, guiding truths and commitments by which the family has always lived. For Solomon it was allegiance to the one true God, Yahweh, and the commandments given to Moses on Mt. Sinai. Following from that we understand "the way" through our faith in Jesus Christ as we confess it in the Creeds of the Christian Church. It is not coincidental that Jesus followers in the early Church were called People of The Way. It is these that are the guiding truths which apply whether young or old. It is these by which parents seek to live themselves and convey to their children.

Life in the way used here extends into all eternity. It is our earthly life extending through all of the years granted us on earth from birth to physical death. Life, however, doesn't end at physical death. Life extends through all eternity. So the training we are responsible for applies to all of our daily temporal activities which also prepare us to live and grow in eternity. Thus the book title *Not For This Life Only*.

A child may be interested in technical or mechanical fields, in musical or artistic fields. They may change their minds a dozen times throughout the growing years, but the same values of a Christ centered life applies to them all. Whether an engineer, a business man, or a government employee, the same values govern their honest and wise behavior. Since our temporal employment takes place in a non-Christian world it is possible that our values may conflict with the world in which we work. We certainly do not seek conflict, or crusade to change all the wrong values around us. Yet, because of our first allegiance to the Lord Jesus Christ we are confronted with a question. Are we willing to live by our Christian values even if there is a personal cost? Whatever our chosen pursuit, be it sales clerk or college professor, our life is to serve others and to grow in our Lord by living The Way He has shown us. By this we have a depth of peace now even if we must suffer some earthly loss, and a joy that extends that extends into eternity.

The Potter and The Clay

God did created us. He is the Potter and we are His clay. Just like my choosing the piece of wood for a cabinet, or the designers of a space exploration system, the maker chooses the way it must be done. We've already noted that human beings and the whole of what we call nature is the most complex of all systems. It is The Potter, Our Maker, who alone has the right to determine our design. It is He who had designed The Way in which we will find the best and longest life possible.

The account of our creation in Genesis chapter one says "God created man in His own image, in the image of God He created him; male and female He created them. God blessed them; and God said to them, "Be fruitful and multiply, and fill the earth, and subdue it; and rule over the fish of the sea and over the birds of the sky and over every living thing that moves on the earth. .....God saw all that He had made, and behold, it was very good." (See vss. 26-31) God created two genders, male and female, that reflect His image. They were to join together in a marital union being fruitful in childbearing. As Genesis chapter two explains the man and woman were suited for each other, there was no sin, nothing shameful in their lives to keep them apart. They had all that we call good and beautiful and without cost. There was only one law, one restriction. They must not eat from the one tree, "from the tree of the knowledge of good and evil you shall not eat". (2:17) They were not told why they should not eat of it, only that there was a penalty if they did. "For in the day that you eat from it you will surely die."

This was a matter of trust for them. They didn't know what evil was. They had no contrast between something good and something not good. They were surrounded by beauty, and a perfection that God, Himself, declared to be "very good". Were they willing to trust their Creator enough to follow His instruction even if they didn't fully understand the reason? One of our seminary professors remarked that every time Adam, in obedience, walked past that Tree he was worshiping God. Our obedience, our willingness to walk in The Way, is part of our worship.

It is The Way that Satan has sought to destroy. He begins by contradicting God. "You surely will not die." He was essentially saying God was deceiving them. "For God knows that in the day your eat from it your eyes will be opened, and you will be like God, knowing good and evil!"(Genesis 3:4-5) The first man and woman gave in to the temptation, eating of the forbidden fruit, and immediately felt the depth of shame within.

God was not deceiving them. They had separated themselves from their Maker. They received the result of that separation, spiritual and in time physical death. We have inherited that result down to this day.

Death and Resurrection Within Us

Our fast paced, technological and scientific world mitigates against our having the child like faith that Jesus sought for all believers.[3] But we can grow into it. God uses various situations, and places us in circumstances in life, where we can grow and mature. Instead of responding to challenges out of our human nature, which is fallen, we can seek God's help to respond out of Jesus' nature. That is what the remainder of this book is about. We will not do it perfectly. We will not do it consistently. We will, as with all growth, have growing pains, but we will grow. The only failure is being complacent, being satisfied where we are, and not realizing the greatness to which God calls us. J.D. may well find happiness for himself during his lifetime, but he will never know the joy that could be his in Jesus Christ.

Living our lives with Jesus means that we follow Him through to death and resurrection. He loves us enough to take our hand as we progressively die to each part of our old nature, and are raised again to a new life in His nature. In this way we reflect a little more of God's image in which we were originally created.

God's richest blessing as we continue our journey together, upholding one another in prayer. I.F.S.

Notes

[1]   William H. Marnell, Man-Made Morals: Four Philosophies That Shaped America, page 179

[2]   Peter Kreeft, C.S.Lewis For The Third Millennium, page 46 & 48

[3]   Mark 10:15

CONTENTS

CHAPTER 1

Destined For Eternity

"I say to you, love your enemies and pray for those who persecute you..." These are Jesus' words in the Sermon on the Mount recorded in Matthew 5:44. They are hard words for us to follow, along with the other words that preceded it in verses 39 to 43 - "turn the other cheek", "give someone your cloak who has already taken your coat", "go the second mile if forced to go the first". There are many other expressions about washing people's feet, and being willing to be last instead of first. This is not natural. It goes against our grain. It strikes at all we believe to be just and fair. But Jesus did say these things, so how do we do them? This will be the question we seek to answer in these chapters.

The question is not only how we do them, but why we should. The title *Not For This Life Only* indicates that there is something beyond this life that gives a reason for living our present life by certain standards and values. As Christians, we believe that those values are established by Almighty God, that they are given for our good, and that He works in us to form them. All this we will examine.

Here to seek God. Acts 17:26 – 27

The Apostle Paul was speaking to the philosophers in Athens. He had seen a monument dedicated to "an Unknown God". This gave him the opening he needed to proclaim the truth about our God, the one true God. He explained that God is the Creator of all things and said:

"He made from one man every nation of mankind to live on all the face of the earth, having determined their appointed times and the boundaries of their habitation, that they would seek God, if perhaps they might grope for Him and find Him, though He is not far from each one of us;..."

(verses 26&27)

Look at what is being said here. God created us. He planned creation even determining how people would inhabit the whole earth. But then it says that he did this "so that men would seek him...and perhaps reach out for him...and find him". God has placed us on earth to get to know him as God. There is a mystery in this. For as Paul says, "now we see but a poor reflection". (I Corinthians 13:12 NIV) This must require learning to know God by faith. If God wanted us to know Him, why wouldn't He just make Himself visible, show us some miracles, and reveal who He is? Of course, He did this in Jesus Christ, but there must be something much deeper being said here in this task of seeking to know God. Jesus later said to Thomas, "blessed are those who did not see and yet believed" (John 20:29). Learning to know God by faith is our task on earth, but to know Him involves a lot more than just believing that Jesus exists, and that He gave His life for our redemption.

A Shallow View of Life

Too many Christians have a shallow view of what the Christian life consists. Often Godliness is equated with a good moral life, yet even pagans can live good moral lives. The teachings of Islam give many moral directions, but they are certainly far different in their doctrines from what Christianity teaches. For many Christians, living the Christian life looks something like this:

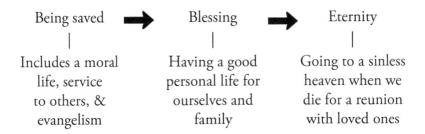

Being saved ➡ Blessing ➡ Eternity

| Includes a moral life, service to others, & evangelism | Having a good personal life for ourselves and family | Going to a sinless heaven when we die for a reunion with loved ones |

I don't mean to be overly simplistic here, or to indicate that these things are wrong in themselves. All of these aspects of the Christian life are true and good, but I don't believe they are complete. I don't believe these are what Paul was trying to indicate to the Athenians by *seeking God*. The translation makes the expression quite strong: "if perhaps they might *grope for Him*, and find Him". Even knowing the truth of the Gospel, and loving Jesus for all that He has done for us, is not the whole of our purpose for our time on earth. Nor, I might add with fear and trepidation, is evangelism our purpose for being on earth. While as important, and vital, as these things are, they are not the primary attributes God is looking for in Christian believers. We are living *Not For This Life Only*.

To Know Him

In the Old Testament the word "know" was used for the union between a man and woman. In Genesis 4:1 it says, "Adam knew his wife Eve and she conceived and bore Cain."(KJV & NKJV) Other Bible versions will say "Adam lay with his wife" (NIV), or "Adam had relations with his wife" (NAS). This is the most intimate of all relationships, and the word *know* includes more than the sexual act. The relationship of husband and wife is becoming *one flesh*, which is a deep and intimate knowledge of each other. This is a knowledge that includes not just the physical, but all aspects of the other's nature. In both Old and New Testaments, the model of marriage is used to prefigure God and Israel, and Christ and the Church. This is why groping for God and finding Him is deeper than just knowing the truth of the Gospel. It takes a whole married life to get to know one's mate. So, with our Lord, learning to know Him, to know His nature and wanting to be like Him, is our task that continues throughout life. In the next chapters, we will be working toward understanding and desiring God's nature so that we are fitted for God's purpose in eternity.

The Eternal Time Line

God is beyond time. "With the Lord one day is like a thousand years, and a thousand years like one day." (2 Peter 3:8) But if we represent God's existence as a time line, it might look something like this:

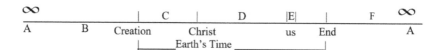

A. The symbol for infinity. God, our Triune God, Father, Son, and Holy Spirit, has no beginning and no end. This boggles the mind, but it is the truth we believe about God. He is infinite, and His realm is called eternity.

B. At some point in God's eternity He created the three great archangels, Gabriel, Michael, and Lucifer. Further, He created the seraphim, and cherubim, all the host of heaven that we read about, for example, in Isaiah 6, when the prophet had the vision of the throne of God. Eternity, before creation, was filled with myriads of myriads of heavenly beings. All of this creativity was motivated by the outflow of God's love. "God is love" (1John 4:8), and the very nature of agape is to flow out in giving life to others.

Creation: At a point in God's eternal purpose, He planned a physical creation, all that we know as the cosmos. This was altogether different than anything He had made before. He was creating a being called man. A being made in His image, yet greatly limited compared to the heavenly beings. He was made "a little lower than the heavenly beings" (Psalm 8:5 NIV), but he was to have a special, and ultimately higher place in God's created order. We are told by St. Paul that "we will judge angels" (1Corinthians 6:3). We have no concept of what this means, but it is a truth that Scripture conveys. I believe this is the reason for Lucifer's rebellion from God, and his downfall. He was the glorious covering cherub. He was the angel of light, one of the first three created beings. How could God...why would God, create this nothing of a weak, limited human, and destine him to be greater than himself? His pride was his downfall, and he has infected the human race with that pride to this very day. Creation continues until the End when Peter tells us that the "earth and its works will be burned up" (2 Peter 3:10). There will be a new and heavenly city of God. Whether this is 7000 years of sacred history, or the 15 billion years scientists tell us the cosmos has existed, it is still a very small span in eternity.

C. Between creation and the birth of Christ, we have all of the events we read about in the Old Testament. The Fall, the promised Redeemer, the Flood and Noah, the journey of the stiff-necked Hebrews under Moses, The Kingdoms of Judah, Israel and their idolatry, their captivity in Babylon and return to rebuild Jerusalem, and then all of the events in the so called intertestamental period up to the coming of Christ. Man has been an awfully lot of trouble to God. God could have given up and destroyed him numerous times. He placed man in Paradise, and man rebelled. Yet God promised a Redeemer.[1] Mankind became so wicked that God sent a flood to destroy them all. Yet God used one faithful man, Noah, to preserve the race.[2] The Hebrews grumbled so much against God while coming out of Egypt that he was ready to destroy them all, and start the race over with Moses.[3] Only Moses intercessions preserved the Hebrew people. Man's nature was sinful to the core. Yet God, Himself, became incarnate in order to redeem the human race. Why did God persist?

D. Even after the atonement and glorious resurrection, Pentecost and the giving of the Holy Spirit, man has still displayed his dullness, his lack of faith, and his sinful nature, to this day. Man is an incredible amount of trouble to God, but God has never given up on his creation. What is it in the *seeking and perhaps finding* that is so important to Him?

E. At a point between Christ and the End, God created you and me. Between Creation and the End, He made every human that has ever lived. We are granted a span of years - sixty, seventy, eighty, ninety, whatever the length. Your span of years, in the midst of earth's history, has meaning and purpose for God. God seeks to work with each of us day by day, gently seeking to draw us more deeply into His life.

F. We have eternal life with God in Christ. We will be an occupant of His eternity. What is He seeking to do with us now in our earthly days that will have a purpose for Him in eternity? I Corinthians 13 teaches us about the nature of love, and we are told that "faith, hope and love remain" eternally. What is our purpose now in learning to live in these three characteristics that will serve God forever? I want you to see that your life has a far greater purpose in God's plan, and that he has placed you on this earth to learn and grow in that purpose, preparing you for your eternal calling. Paul, quoting from Isaiah, has said, "things which eye has not seen and ear has not heard...all that God has prepared for those who love Him" (1Corinthians 2:9).

God works in our life so we learn to know Him

God works with us day by day, circumstance by circumstance, to help us find and grow in his purpose. It is hard for us to understand how God is using circumstances when we are going through them, but we can grow in responding to circumstances with the nature of Christ, and this is what He desires. Let's look at what Jeremiah said to his people that were about to go into captivity:

> "For thus says the LORD, 'When seventy years have been completed for Babylon, I will visit you and fulfill My good word to you, to bring you back to this place. 'For I know the plans that I have for you,' declares the LORD, 'plans for welfare and not for calamity to give you a future and a hope. 'Then you will call upon Me and come and pray to Me, and I will listen to you. 'You will seek Me and find Me when you search for Me with all your heart. 'I will be found by you,' declares the LORD, 'and I will restore your fortunes and will gather you from all the nations and from all the places where I have driven you,' declares the LORD, 'and I will bring you back to the place from where I sent you into exile.'"

> (Jeremiah 29:10-14)

God told Israel that, because of their sins, they would have to go into captivity in Babylon for 70 years. This would not be a happy prospect for any people. It was difficult to be uprooted from home, possessions, and familiar land. It was a circumstance they had to endure, and over the70 years many died in that foreign land. Even so, God gave them the promise of their return, and that he had plans for their good. Here, also,

He emphasized the need for them to seek for him with all their hearts. In this difficult circumstance, they had the possibility of growing and coming closer to their Lord.

Knowing God is knowing and understanding his nature. John has told us that God is love. He has demonstrated his nature of love throughout the Scriptures, and it is important for us to understand what it means when we say this simple phrase *God is love*.

Agape - The Highest of the Four Loves, and the Nature of God

Our English language is often limited in its expressions compared to other languages. We have the word *love* which is used in so many different ways, everything from I love pancakes, to I love you, dear. And there are so many distortions in today's world of the concept of love. In the Greek language of the New Testament there are four words that are all translated love:

Eros - the erotic and sexual love,
Phylia - brotherly love, the deep bond between friends,
Storge - is similar to phylia, affection, and includes family love, such as the love of a parent toward a child
Agape - the pure self-sacrificing love displayed in God's nature.

All of the expressions of love are good and have their place, but only agape love seeks no gain. It is love that continues even when there is no response, or even a negative response, from one loved. It is the love that exists within the Holy Trinity, and the motivating power in all creation. It is love reserved for human beings, and would not be spoken of toward animals or inanimate objects. Agape is the love we spoke about in the beginning that can love an enemy. Agape is the pure nature of God, and the nature that God seeks to bring about in our lives.

In Matthew 22:37-39, Jesus tells us where this love is displayed. We call them the two great commandments. I write it here inserting the correct Greek word for love. You shall *"agapaho the Lord your God with all your heart and with all your soul and with all your mind.' This is the great and foremost commandment. And the second is like it: 'You shall Agapaho your neighbor as yourself.'"* Agape is the love that we are to show toward both our God and our neighbor.

I very much appreciate the description of love that C. S. Lewis gives in his fantasy writing *The Screwtape Letters.* This series of letters are written from the point of view of a senior devil instructing his junior in the ways of tempting and overcoming the human to whom he is assigned. In this passage he is speaking of the Enemy's (God's) nature of humility and love.[4]

Screwtrape continues his examination of the virtue of Humility:

To anticipate the Enemy's strategy, we must consider His aims. The Enemy wants to bring the man to a state of mind in which he could design the best cathedral in the world, and know it to be the best, and rejoice in the fact, without being any more (or less) or otherwise glad at having done it than he would be if it had been come by another. The Enemy wants him in the end, to be so free from any bias in his own favor that he can rejoice in his own talents as frankly and gratefully as in his neighbour's talents - or in a sunrise, an elephant, or a waterfall. He wants each man, in the long run, to be able to recognize all creatures (even himself) as glorious and excellent things. He wants to kill their animal self-love as soon as possible; but it is His long-term policy, I fear, to restore to them a new kind of self-love - a charity and gratitude for all selves, including their own; when they have really learned to love their neighbours as themselves, they will be allowed to love themselves as their neighbours. For we must never forget what is the most repellent and inexplicable trait in our Enemy; He really loves the hairless bipeds He has created and always gives back to them with His right hand what He has taken away with His left.

As Christians, as believers in the Lord Jesus Christ, as forgiven and cleansed sinners, as recipients of His great grace, and His agape love, it is our desire to serve and please Him with our lives. The question for us is: what is the life that brings the most glory to God? It is a life that fulfills the purpose for which we were created. God created us in his image, which we lost in the rebellion of our first parents, and which is lost in natural man to this day. It is only restored by God's grace through faith in Jesus Christ. And once restored, God desires that we grow in that image throughout life. The point of our life on earth is learning, through all circumstances, to live out God's image, God's nature of agape, self sacrificing, love. This is the life that has eternal value and a real purpose for our Lord in His Kingdom.

Notes

[1]   Genesis 3:15

[2]   Genesis 6:8

[3]   Deuteronomy 9:14

[4]   C. S. Lewis, The Screwtape Letters, (New York, Simon & Schuster, Touchstone Books, 1996)

CHAPTER 2

What is Man That You Are Mindful of Him?

God's nature is made known through the Church

In the Old Testament, God set a people apart, the Hebrews, intending they ultimately carry the truth of God's grace to the world. This was the covenant that God made with Abraham in Genesis 12:1-3, that Abraham and his descendants would be blessed so that they could be a blessing to all the nations of the earth. With the advent of Christ, that covenant was expanded to include all who believe in the Lord Jesus. Through the Church, the Gospel of God's grace is to be carried to the world. Paul shows this when he writes to the Ephesian church.

> "Although I am less than the least of all God's people, this grace was given me: to preach to the Gentiles the unsearchable riches of Christ, and to make plain to everyone the administration of this mystery, which for ages past was kept hidden in God, who created all things. His intent was that now, through the church, the manifold wisdom of God should be made known to the rulers and authorities in the heavenly realms, according to his eternal purpose which he accomplished in Christ Jesus our Lord."
>
> Ephesians 3: 8-11

* Paul is to preach the unsearchable riches of Christ. This is the Good News of our salvation by grace through faith in Jesus Christ. It is also the nature of the person of Jesus, the nature of the Godhead expressed in sacrificial love, forgiveness, patience, meekness, and all his other attributes. This is the unending depth of the riches of Christ Jesus. It is this that the Church is to learn and to reflect.

* It is the mystery hidden for ages and now revealed in the Church. This is the wonderful nature of God which was not fully seen until the appearing of Jesus. It is revealed in the Church, but the Church is a general body of believers. The local manifestation of God's nature is to be seen in each individual Christian.

* Through the Church, the manifold wisdom of God is made known to the rulers and authorities in the heavenly realms. God brought mankind into being as the highest of his created order, ordained with a divine purpose for eternity. Each of God's beings has a special reason for their creation - the archangels, the angels, the seraphim and cherubim, all the principalities, powers, realms and dimensions, all have a special purpose in God's eternal order. And man, the weakest of created beings, is to occupy the highest place in that order. Man is created to share the very nature and image of Almighty God. This is not said about any other created beings. The mystery revealed to the *heavenly realms* is why God uses the weakest of created beings to display the fullest of his nature.

God's Nature is Humble, and Meek

The Apostle Peter wrote,

> "It was revealed to them (the Old Testament prophets) that they were not serving themselves, but you, in these things which now have been announced to you through those who reached the gospel to you by the Holy Spirit sent from heaven--things into which angels long to look."
>
> 1 Peter 1:12

What things could even angels long to look? As we understand angels, they are glorious heavenly beings serving in the presence of God. Yet they are in no way equal to God, and are limited in their understanding of the full nature of God. We saw this in the first chapter where Lucifer, the glorious archangel, didn't understand why God would create a being far weaker than himself to ultimately rule over him. The nature of God is an awesome mystery. God who is almighty, yet chooses to reveal himself in humility and gentleness. Jesus, the Son, the second person of the Holy Trinity, is the perfect reflection of God's nature. God is one undivided being, yet chooses to reveal himself in three persons. What we see in Jesus we understand of God's nature. The more we draw near to the nature of Jesus the more we want to bow in humble worship of Almighty God.

Jesus said of Himself, "Take my yoke upon you and learn from me, for I am gentle and humble in heart, and you will find rest for your souls." (Matthew 11:29) *Gentle and humble in heart.* That is amazing! The One who also said, "all authority in heaven and on earth has been given to me" (Matthew 28:18), is at the same time gentle and humble. This is vitally important for our understanding of God. God is almighty, all powerful, yet at the same time His nature is humble, and meek. We have difficulty understanding these words as being applied to God, but the point is that they speak of a nature that is the opposite of pride, of self-exaltation, which is the nature that Satan displays.

Two Greek words in Matthew 11:29 are variously translated gentle, humble, lowly, or meek. In our English context we attach the idea of weakness to these characteristics. Such is not the case at all. The word meek speaks of being steadfast in one's position, of knowing the authority one has, but not having to flaunt it. Moses was called the meekest of man, but he was by no means weak, or in any way shrinking before opposition. These are the characteristic that are to grow in us as Paul taught. "Your attitude should be the same as that of Christ Jesus: who, being in the very nature of God, did not consider equality with God something to be grasped, but made himself nothing...he humbled himself..." (Philipplians 2:6–8).

What is displayed in these characteristics is the awesome power of sacrificial love, a power greater than any force on earth. This is what is to be displayed in the weakness of mankind. It is this that even the heavenly realms don't fully comprehend. Nor do we fully comprehend all that the deep nature of God means. It is reflected in the Old Testament Hebrew word, *hesed*, translated *loving kindness, or steadfast love*, and in the New Testament Greek by *agape*. It is this into which mankind was created to grow, and to display in both the earthly and the heavenly realms, as Jesus' life is lived through them.

Love is the law of the universe, or rather, the Kingdom of God

It is truly amazing why this should be. I John 4:16 has told us that God is love. Did you ever let your mind delve into this? Why should the nature of the Almighty be love? Why would He not just as well be The Force as Star Wars pictures Him? Or why not simply nirvana in the Buddhist concept? This becomes a deep philosophical question that could be endlessly debated. Why is God's nature love? There are many things in our world that seem to speak to the contrary. So many wars. So many tragedies. The question people sometimes confront Christians with - how could a good God allow...? Yet, He is love! We could discuss the philosophy for ages and not be satisfied. But God has shown us proof of His love in Jesus Christ. "God demonstrates his own love toward us, in that while we were yet sinners, Christ died for us." (Romans 5:8) We will not answer all of the why questions on this earth. We can only point to the greatest of all demonstrations of love in Jesus Christ. Our only response to this is gratitude, worship, and trust.

Seven Thousand who have not bowed the knee to Baal

God uses the Church to express his nature of love. God is working in people to help them become like him, humble, lowly, and meek, thus expressing his self-sacrificing love. These are qualities that will be needed and used in the heavenly realms yet unseen. Unfortunately, due to the shallow state of the church today, most have a very superficial understanding of what God really desires in mankind. It was all in Jesus' words, especially in his so called hard sayings. But too often we rationalize them away, and don't face the truth they contain.

Scripture gives us a description of the nature of the Church in the last times before the Lord's return. All of the time following the death and resurrection of our Lord is considered the last days. We do not try to set dates on our Lord's return, but to understand the kind of people he seeks to develop for His Kingdom in these last days. I believe many will be saved, as the thief on the cross, but not many will grow to the maturity God desires. The Old Testament speaks of the 7000, out of all Israel, who have not bowed the knee to Baal (1 Kings 19:18), or the remnant who is faithful out of Israel. (Isaiah 10:20 and others.) In the New Testament there is a distinction between the wise and foolish virgins, and the five other groups spoken of in Matthew 25. And, as we will see in a few paragraphs later on, there is a difference between those whose works are gold, silver, and precious stones or wood, hay, and stubble, as Paul describes in 1 Corinthians 3:12-15.

Remember, I am always making a distinction in this writing between the wonderful grace of salvation, and the work that God seeks to do in the heart over a lifetime of maturing believers. It is in this latter work that we exercise great choice either to yield to, or resist, the guiding hand of the Lord. It is the same with children born into our family. They don't have a choice about being born or being loved by the parents, but they have wide choices about following parent's guidance and becoming mature and responsible adults. We have seen all too many make the wrong choices.

What are the Right Choices?

The last two churches spoken of in Revelation 3 are characteristic of the concluding period before the Lord's return. Philadelphia is one of only two churches in the list of seven that receives no rebuke from the Lord. Jesus says of this church, "I know that you have little strength, yet you have kept my word and not denied my name." Revelation 3:8 NIV

The church at Laodicea, on the other hand, receives a rebuke and a sharp warning.

> "I know your deeds, that you are neither cold nor hot; I wish that you were cold or hot. So because you are lukewarm, and neither hot nor cold, I will spit you out of My mouth."

> Revelation 3:15-16

This, unfortunately, is the shallowness of many churches and Christians today. And in saying this I never mean to set myself or my church up as being any different. We are certainly not ones who have all wisdom. I simply say it to lament the state of the whole Church today, and encourage us to desire the very best that God has for us.

> "because you say, 'I am rich, and have become wealthy, and have need of nothing,' and you do not know that you are wretched and miserable and poor and blind and naked."

> Revelation 3:17

This is why the Lord rejects this church. They have no concept of their true condition, or of the love that the Lord desired for them. However, He does give them an alternative.

"I advise you to buy from Me gold refined by fire so that you may become rich, and white garments so that you may clothe yourself, and that the shame of your nakedness will not be revealed; and eye salve to anoint your eyes so that you may see."

Revelation 3:18

Everything comes from Jesus. In seeking Him we find life. *Gold refined by fire*, refers to God's eternal truth, God's values, nature, and life. It is refined into our lives by the trials and circumstances of life. The white robe to hide the *shame of our nakedness* is the robe of Christ's righteousness won for us at Calvary. It is the robe that the father put around the Prodigal son to cover the dirt of the pigsty. (Luke 15:11-14) This is the glorious truth of forgiveness and life in Jesus Christ, and the wonderful depth of his love. *Eye salve anoints the eye* is to give us sight. This is not physical sight, but the work of God's Spirit giving discernment to understand the true condition of the Church and the world. It is what God is looking for today.

We have little strength today. We are not going to change the state of the Church. Ecumenical dialogue is fine, but we are not going to change the Church by mergers. All mergers become more liberal and further away from God's Word. God seeks those few who are willing to see and understand the Church's condition, and hunger to live more in the nature of Christ's love. This is growing into maturity, and beginning to see things through God's eyes.

A People Who Know How to Repent

Jesus continues: in Revelation 3:19 " Those whom I love, I reprove and discipline; therefore be zealous and repent." This is the training in each life. God is treating us as his sons and daughters. (Hebrews 12:7) He is looking for those who are willing to repent. Repentance is a word we treat far too lightly. Yes, when we do or say something that we know is wrong we confess it to God, asking forgiveness. This is personal repentance, and something we need regularly. But repentance is more than this. The great prayers of Scripture were both personal <u>and</u> corporate. Prayer was made "for my sins *and* the sins of my people." (Daniel 9 and others) This is the point of the *eye salve*, so that we can see the true condition of our people, and come before God in repentance, crying out for his healing and renewal, ultimately in the return of our Lord Jesus Christ.

We must realize that we are one church in God's eyes. We are one people who have taken the name of Christian for ourselves. While we live in the tragic necessity of thousands of different Christian denominations this is not the church Christ intended when he prayed asking the Father that "they may be one even as we are one." (John 17:22)

We see things happening within the Church, acceptance of LGBTQ lifestyles as normal even to be celebrated; theologies and worship that reject the atoning work of Christ; changing the Scriptures to make them conform to modern thought, or rejecting them in general as God revealed word; and many more such deviations from God's truth. These should cut us to the heart, and bring us to our knees before God. These things separate people from the love of the Lord. We may not have committed these sins directly, but we are a part of the Church that has. God is simply looking for people today who can see and cry out to him in repentance for the whole Christian church.

God Seeks The Few Who Are Willing

Jesus continues His message to the Laodicean church saying,

> "Behold, I stand at the door and knock; if anyone hears My voice and opens the door, I will come in to him and will dine with him, and he with Me."
>
> (Revelation 3:20)

This verse is often used as a call to salvation. That certainly is an application; however, it is also more than this. It is an invitation to any Christian who will hear Christ's words, and be willing to submit to God's maturing hand, being willing to have him work verses 18 and 19 deeply in their life. These are the seven thousand who have not bowed the knee to Baal. It comes with a promise in verse 21, "He who overcomes, I will grant to him to sit down with Me on My throne, as I also overcame and sat down with My Father on His throne." This is the great promise of God's grace, to share the throne of God. We don't have a concept of what this really means, but it is a glorious promise, and a reward for all who overcome, for all who desire true fellowship with God and yield to the Father's guiding hand throughout life.

What is man? the eighth Psalm ponders. What is the awesome position we are being trained to occupy in eternity? He will reveal it to us in time, but for now we are to learn to know and to want God's nature of pure love formed more fully in our own lives. It is reflecting the nature of Christ's love to our world that makes us different and unique.

Love Witnesses to the World

Cal Thomas was very active in the Moral Majority in the early 1980s. The Moral Majority sought to influence society through participating strongly in the political process. Thomas left the organization in 1985 with a complete change in direction to his thinking. He realized that participation in politics was not the right avenue for Christians to influence social change. Since then he has raised the ire of many conservative Evangelicals who are committed to that process. In 2000 he wrote a book entitled *Blinded By Might* explaining his position. Following the 2008 presidential election, in which both parties actively courted the Evangelical vote, he made a similar point in a newspaper editorial.

"Social movements that relied mainly on political power to enforce a conservative moral code weren't anywhere near as successful as those that focused on changing hearts...If results are what conservative Evangelicals want, they already have a model. It is contained in the life and commands of Jesus of Nazareth. Suppose millions of conservative Evangelicals engaged in an old and proven type of radical behavior. Suppose they followed the admonition of Jesus to 'love your enemies, pray for those who persecute you, feed the hungry, clothe the naked, visit those in prison, and care for widows and orphans,' not as ends, as so many liberals do by using government, but as a means of demonstrating God's love for the whole person in order that people might seek Him?"[1]

It is this *heart change* that God seeks in all of us. This is living in God's agape love which is of ultimate value in life now and for eternity. This is the kind of life of mature love that touches and changes lives around us.

Notes

[1]   Cal Thomas, Religious Right R.I.P., November 5, 2008, Tribune Media Service, Inc Buffalo, N.Y.

CHAPTER 3

The Earth is Our Apprenticeship for Rulership

The Great Questions of Life

Overall these chapters will be answering the three great questions of life: *Who am I? Why am I here? Where am I going?* These are questions each person must ponder at some point in life, though in our day, I think they are pushed aside. We live in the *whatever* generation marked by the lack of absolute values, and the main concerns for living are those things that we think will bring happiness. It is possible to deaden the impact of these questions with the attitude, *eat, drink, and be merry, for tomorrow we die,* though we never really say it quite that way. However, if we are at all serious about life, then we must think about these questions.

To the first question: who am I? we emphasize over and over what our Gospel teaches. You are a child of God for Jesus' sake. You are redeemed. You have been bought with the price of Jesus' blood. This is something that we hold on to. Never forget it. Never doubt it. This is who you are.

It is the second and third questions we want to understand clearly, especially as Christians. There is a great deal involved with God's purpose for us in life as we saw in the pondering question of Psalm 8. We can't simply take the shallow view of our faith that we spoke of in the first chapter.

When a prince is born into a royal household, his life is marked with that destiny from the beginning. All of his upbringing, all of his education, the whole course of his life, is guided toward the day when he will advance to the throne. So it is to be with the baptized people of God.

Dying to Reign

Paul writing to his spiritual son, Timothy, said,

"it is a trustworthy statement: For if we died with Him, we will also live with Him; If we endure, we will also reign with Him; If we deny Him, He also will deny us."

2 Timothy 2:11-12

To die with Christ is to die to our old nature, and to desire Christ to form his nature more fully in us. Jesus pointed out that suffering would be involved in this world, and if we endure, we shall reign with Him. What does it mean to reign? We think of a king or sovereign of a country. This is what Paul is saying we are called to do with Christ. We don't know all that this means in the heavenly realm, but in some way we are to reign with Christ.

Revelation 20:6 says,

"Blessed and holy is the one who has a part in the first resurrection; over these the second death has no power, but they will be priests of God and of Christ and will reign with Him for a thousand years."

Here again we are taught that we are to reign with Christ. My emphasis is not the so called millennial period, but rather our call to reign. In the Old Testament God speaking to Israel said,

"Now then, if you will indeed obey My voice and keep My covenant, then you shall be My own possession among all the peoples, for all the earth is Mine; and you shall be to Me a kingdom of priests and a holy nation.."

Exodus 19:5-6

The Hebrew word translated *possessions* speaks of something of wealth or a treasure. This would be in a similar fashion as we might refer to a son or daughter as a treasure.

These are God's words through Moses, but they also speak to us. We are people of the New Covenant in Christ. We are God's own possession, and we are called to be a kingdom of priests to our God. In Matthew Chapter ten Jesus gave his disciples instructions before he sent them out to minister in the towns of Israel. He said,

> "A disciple is not above his teacher nor a slave above his master. It is enough for the disciple that he becomes like his teacher and the slave like his master."
>
> Matthew 10:24-25

Much of eternity remains a mystery, but numerous Scripture references point to our calling to occupy a holy position with Christ. In some yet unknown way we are called to reign with Christ, serving in his glorious kingdom as he directs.

We then have a beginning answer to the second great question. *Why are we here?* We have a high calling from God, and we are being apprenticed for rulership in Christ's Kingdom. We need to see what is involved in this. Then this will begin to make sense, and give some reason to the things that happen to us in life. We are just like youngsters in middle school who have to learn things that, at the time, they see no application in their life, but years later they do see the reason, and are glad they had to learn them. Our Lord is working to train us through all of the times, situations, and trials we go through now.

Invited to a Banquet - Called to Occupy a Mansion

Revelation 19:7-9 speaks of the Marriage Supper of the Lamb.

"Let us rejoice and be glad and give the glory to Him, for the marriage of the Lamb has come and His bride has made herself ready.' It was given to her to clothe herself in fine linen, bright and clean; for the fine linen is the righteous acts of the saints. Then he said to me, 'Write, Blessed are those who are invited to the marriage supper of the Lamb.' And he said to me, 'These are true words of God.'"

All of these expressions are human images that try to explain heavenly truths. But, as with Paul being caught up into the third heaven, there are no adequate words to fully explain them.

It is important to understand that God desires all people to be saved, and he wants as many as are willing, to grow into maturity. He has given us a wide latitude in our response to his call. God would like all people to share in rulership in His Kingdom, but not all will. Many will choose other paths. God's Kingdom is infinitely vast and there are many levels and degrees. Jesus said, "in My Father's house are many dwelling places". (John 14:2)

You will find that I use the word *kingdom* often, rather than *heaven*. This is intentional. Heaven is a term that can carry all kinds of false impressions. It is displayed in cartoons as billowy clouds and pearly gates, or in sentimental talk as a blissful place of reunion. Kingdom, on the other hand, speaks of a multidimensional realm with a throne at the center and many degrees of authority under the King. It is something of what Jesus meant by the many mansions, or dwelling places. There are different dwelling places for different degrees of maturity. During our lifetime apprenticeship on earth, we are to understand something of the nature of God's Kingdom, and desire that God train us as much as possible, preparing us for the dwelling place he has planned.

I believe there will be growth in heaven. We will learn and be further matured from our contact with the saints that have gone before us, but earth is a special training ground where we are to learn by faith and not by sight. This is certainly no doctrine of a purgatory where sins must yet be dealt with. That has occurred once for all time at the cross. Forgiveness is complete in Jesus Christ. But this understanding does recognize the infinite extent of God's eternal Kingdom, and our growth in that Kingdom

In Matthew 25, Jesus tells three parables about the Kingdom. This further illuminates truths about these *mansions* or *dwelling places*. The parables are about the Wise and Foolish Virgins, the Three Servants, and the Sheep and Goats. All three parables are to be taken together as a picture of the Kingdom. In the three, there are seven groups of people. Among these seven, four are rewarded and three are judged. There are degrees of rewards, and degrees of judgment. Some have interpreted these parables as saying that the four rewards are all the same, that is, gaining salvation and heaven. And the people in the three judgments are all sent to hell. I do not believe this is correct. For example, the five wise virgins all get to be with the Lord in the marriage banquet, while the five foolish do not. The five foolish are still virgins, that is pure, but they are rebuked by the Lord for not having sufficient oil. That is not accepting guidance from the Holy Spirit. They are not in hell. They are in a different place in God's Kingdom. Likewise, the five-talent servant, the two- talent servant, and the sheep, each receive a different reward.

It may seem like splitting hairs with a Scriptural interpretation, but it is important to understand that there are many levels and degrees to God's Kingdom. At least our initial place in the Kingdom depends a great deal on our life-long response to our apprenticeship. Certainly, all of heaven, all of God's Kingdom, is glorious and sinless beyond anything we can imagine, but God wants us to desire and strive for the best, allowing Him to work as deeply as possible in our life.

James and John understood this when they asked for one to sit at Jesus' right hand and one to His left in His Kingdom. (Mark 10:37) Jesus did not rebuke them for this desire. He simply said that it was not His to grant, but was in the Father's judgment. Further, on a number of occasions, Jesus selected three of His disciples, Peter, James, and John, for special privileges, for example, witnessing the raising of Jairus' daughter, (Luke 8:51) and going up on the Mount of Transfiguration. (Mark 9:2) This, along with His statement about the Kingdom having many dwelling places, shows us something of the vast, multileveled place that is God's Kingdom.

Answering the Three Questions

There is much more to be said to obtain a depth of understanding, but we now have at least a beginning of the answers to the three great questions of life:

* *Who am I?* - You are a child of God because of the sacrifice of Jesus Christ on Calvary.

* *Why am I here?* - You are here to learn the lessons of sacrificial love and conforming to the nature of Jesus. It is this that God wants to teach you in the depth of your heart, as you walk by faith in Him?

* *Where am I going?* – You are going to occupy God's eternal Kingdom, and to put into His service the lessons of love you have learned here on earth.

A Changed Heart

During our apprenticeship on earth, the Lord works in our hearts to shape us into Christ's nature, and fit us for our place in the Kingdom.

It is what comes from the heart that is central for our Lord. Jesus makes this clear in the Sermon on the Mount by showing that what happens in the heart is as serious as external actions. And in Matthew 5:21-28. Later on in a discussion about what truly defiles a person Jesus states, "for out of the heart come evil thoughts, murders, adulteries, fornications, thefts, false witness, slanders." (Matthew 15:19) It is always God's desire that all people be at the Wedding Banquet, but he leaves a lot up to us in how we respond to the invitation Consider the parable of the wedding banquet.

> "The kingdom of heaven is like a king who prepared a wedding banquet for his son. He sent his servants to those who had been invited to the banquet to tell them to come, but they refused to come. Then he sent some more servants and said, 'Tell those who have been invited that I have prepared my dinner: My oxen and fattened cattle have been butchered, and everything is ready. Come to the wedding banquet.' But they paid no attention and went off—one to his field, another to his business. The rest seized his servants, mistreated them and killed them. The king was enraged. He sent his army and destroyed those murderers and burned their city. Then he said to his servants, 'The wedding banquet is ready, but those I invited did not deserve to come. Go to the street corners and invite to the banquet anyone you find.' So the servants went out into the streets and gathered all the people they could find, both good and bad, and the wedding hall was filled with guests. But when the king came in to see the guests, he noticed a man there who was not wearing wedding clothes. 'Friend,' he asked, 'how did you get in here without wedding clothes?' The man was speechless. Then the king told the attendants, 'Tie him hand and foot, and throw him outside, into the darkness, where there will be weeping and gnashing of teeth.' For many are invited, but few are chosen."
>
> Matthew 22:2-13

We absolutely have our salvation by grace through faith in Jesus Christ, but salvation is just the doorway to the sheep fold. (John 10:7-10) We are called to grow up into Christ. (Ephesians 4:15) It is why Jesus said, "if anyone wishes to come after me, he must deny himself, take up his cross and follow me." (Matthew 16:24), and "whoever wishes to save his life will lose it, but whoever loses his life for My sake, he is the one who will save it." (Luke 9:24) "If anyone *wishes* come after me..." "Whoever *wishes* to save his life..." The followers of Jesus are given many choices about how they respond to his call.

We know this is true, for we all know a variety of believers - true believers in Jesus Christ. Some are open, forgiving, and loving. Others harbor bitterness and hold on to resentments throughout their lives. It is not our place to judge and point fingers at others, but this goes beyond mere personality differences. Jesus works with each of us differently as he did with his first disciples. He is working to cleanse our hearts. We are all sinners. We are all a work in progress, and God seeks to use the circumstances of life to mold and cleanse our hearts, fitting us for his Kingdom, and hopefully the Marriage Supper of the Lamb. Whatever glory that actually means in the reality of the kingdom of heaven it is a beauty, joy, and goodness beyond measure. (See 2 Corinthian 12:2-4)

Our purpose on earth is seen in the context of giving up one's life. Progressively dying to self and being raised to new life in Christ. (Romans 6:3-4) This begins with our baptism and continues throughout life. It is all a work of God's grace as he calls us to yield to his shaping hands.

CHAPTER 4

No Pain, No Gain

Why do bad things happen to good people?

This is a question most of us struggle with at one time or another. It has driven people to despair, even to rejection of God. Many books have been written trying to explain it. Yet, it remains a question we cannot fully answer. We only hope to see more clearly when we get to heaven. But for the moment we need to look more carefully at the question itself. We are asking about things happening to *good people*, but this is a misnomer. Jesus said to the young man who called Him "good teacher", "why do you call me good? No one is good except God alone." (Luke 18:19) And Paul said, "all have sinned and fall short of the glory of God" (Romans 3:23). Both Jesus and Paul are rejecting the term *good* when applied to human nature.

We measure goodness in relative terms. People try to be nice to others, kind, friendly, and outgoing. They are basically honest. When there is a crisis, people pull together. We all know people who are a bit worse than we are. So, good is measured by some general standard we have established. But none of this is what Jesus or Paul is saying. The standard of true goodness is not some generally accepted standard of society. The standard is God, Himself. God is the perfect good by which all is to be measured. In God, there are absolute values of good and bad. By this standard, there is no person on earth who can be called *good* in any absolute terms. So, the question must be modified.

Why Do Bad Things Happen to People?

For this, Genesis chapters one through three give the answer. There was a perfect and very intentional creation by Almighty God. Mankind was made innocent and free from sin in the beginning. At some time after creation, there was a fall from grace, when man and woman rebelled from the command of God. This changed their whole nature. It is always important that we recognize this. There was a perfect creation and a later fall.

I am not concerned, at present, whether the history of the earth was 7000 years or 15 billion years. My emphasis is on the words *intentional creation*. Mankind did not appear by a blind evolutionary act. The teaching of evolution removes God from intentionally creating mankind. This is true even with the teaching of so called theistic evolution, where God is still seen as the creator, but uses the evolutionary process to bring man about. In evolution, God is removed many steps away from intentionally creating man in his image and for his purpose. And if we move God, even a little bit, we also move the standard of his perfect goodness. That is why the teaching of evolution leads to a society that accepts many values as equal or no values at all.

There was an intentional creation, and as God, Himself, said, "It was very good" (Genesis 1:31). It was good, and then, there was a later rebellion from God's command. This is all old history for us, but it is vital in looking at the question we started with. There was a fall from grace, from the innocence of Eden. That fall infected every atom of the universe. We really don't realize the depth of what that rebellion from God has meant, and how it has affected everything. Everything is in chaos - from the individual atom, to the cosmos, to the heart of man. This is very important to understand.

Where there is order, it is God's hand of grace keeping things from falling apart. If God withdraws His hand, things happen. Where there is any order, God is demonstrating His grace. If we ignore God and choose to play with our idols as we have done now over many centuries, if we refuse to follow His instruction, He withdraws His hand a bit and lets some of the chaos reign. Be it drought, tornadoes, fire, or economic problems, we experience problems when we depart from the life our Creator called us to follow.

Why it happens in some places, and to some people, and not to others is only in God's wisdom. It is beyond our knowing. Some people prosper and seem to have all things under control, but that is why we are emphasizing that this present life is only a part of our life eternally. Chaos is in the nature of man, himself. Man learned what evil is. He lost innocence. His nature became filled with pride and self, rather than joy and God. Sin entered the world and has touched every aspect of life from that time forward. But, God was not willing to abandon his creation. He has worked to redeem and restore it ever since. However, things have been made immeasurably more difficult for man from that day until the end of time. So, the short answer to the question, why do bad things happen? They happen because sin has entered the hearts of all people. We confess this in our liturgy saying, "we are by nature sinful and unclean."[1] We live in the midst of a fallen world, and we don't fully realize the depth of our fall.

It is vital that we understand this, for it separates Christianity from all world religions. The Christian Gospel declared that man could not redeem himself, and God acted on his behalf in Jesus Christ. Jesus died on Calvary's cross as the atoning sacrifice for all of our sins. If man is not sinful to the core of his fallen nature, if there is yet some *spark of the divine* in man, if man can work his way to please God or gain his favor, then Jesus' death was not necessary at all. Jesus is reduced in the world's religions to just a moral teacher or a prophet, but certainly not a Redeemer. But this is a totally untenable position considering all that Jesus testified about himself. The Christian doctrine of the sinful nature of man and the necessity of the atoning sacrifice of Christ is a doctrine that the world hates, and a doctrine that the Christian Church cannot yield in any way.

God has provided that atonement in Jesus Christ. He is working daily, by the presence of His Spirit, to change the hearts of people. He cannot simply wink at sin. It must be destroyed. In Jesus, He paid the death penalty that sin deserves, that we all deserve. He took the penalty for all our sins into His own being on Calvary's cross. He took our punishment that we could not possible take ourselves. We deserve hell, eternal separation from God, but He endured it for our sakes. We are no longer under condemnation. (Romans 8:1) We have eternal life by the pure grace of God through faith in Jesus Christ. Now He continues to work in hearts to cleanse out the sin nature that remains. Bad things do happen to people because the sin nature is still active in us and in this world. God allows certain things to happen as they do. They are not random acts, or those of a capricious god.

Are all things from God?

Many questions arise when we are thinking about the sufferings endured in the world: Do all things come from God? Is God in all events? How about cancer and tornados? Is it punishment, discipline, or what? Here we need to make some distinctions. First, remember our fallen nature. All have sinned and fall short of the glory of God. The nature of the whole human race is corrupt. Further, God has given all people a choice about their conduct. Paul writing to Timothy tells us that God "desires all men to be saved and to come to the knowledge of the truth." (1 Timothy 2:4) God's Holy Spirit is at work in the world to call people to himself, but we know that many will use their choices against him. Since God does not want puppets, He doesn't countermand their choices. So there are Hitlers, and abortions, and dads who murder their children. These things are tragic. God does know and care about them more deeply than we can imagine. This is the evil of the world in which we live.

God can use all circumstances for our good.

The writer of Hebrews tells us,

> For those whom the Lord loves He disciplines, and He scourges every son whom He receives. It is for discipline that you endure; God deals with you as with sons; for what son is there whom his father does not discipline?
>
> Hebrews 12:6-7

However, all suffering cannot be said to be God disciplining us. We don't want to look at every cold, or stubbed toe as God disciplining us because we did something wrong. Sometimes, it is direct discipline. Other times it is God using his *pressure* to get us to see something we need to look at in our life. Still other times, recognizing that we live in a fallen world, some things happen through no action or fault of our own.

We can philosophize all day about the whys of evil and suffering, but many of those final answers remain hidden in heaven. We must hold to the truth that God came into this broken world in the person of Jesus Christ. He knows and shares our sorrows. And He remains in this world in the restoring presence of His Holy Spirit. He is a God of love who will bring all things to their right conclusion.

But this is me, Lord! I'm hurting!

How do we deal with the things that come to us personally, whether great or small? Jesus said, "in this world you have tribulation". That is a given. But He immediately followed this by saying, "but take courage, I have overcome the world" (John 16:33). What we face, whether large or small, we face with Jesus. He is working with us to help us respond as he would respond, to respond out of his nature. So there is real godly gain in responding to our pains with the strength God supplies.

God can make pressure from any cause work for us. "We know that God causes all things to work together for the good to those who love God, to those who are called according to His purpose." (Romans 8:28) In this sense, trials, pains, and sufferings are not accidental, but are gifts from God. They can be cherished. For when properly received, they work blessings in us that teach us lessons for eternity. Paul Billheimer, remarked, "No one ever becomes a saint without suffering, because suffering, properly accepted is the pathway to glory."[2]

Leprosy - The Necessity of Pain

Do you know what leprosy is? We hear about it often in the Bible. Leprosy, or Hansen's disease, is a chronic infectious disease caused by bacteria. It is a disease of the upper respiratory tract; skin lesions are the primary external symptom. Left untreated, leprosy can be progressive, causing permanent damage to the skin, nerves, limbs, and eyes. One great problem for a person with leprosy is insensitivity in the limb's extremities. Pain does not trigger an immediate response as in a fully functioning body. God has given physical pain as a protection for our bodies, so that we avoid serious damage. Lepers lack this protection.

Leprosy has its spiritual counterpart. God uses the pains that come to us in life to show us where our life needs healing. God very much wants to bless us. A life of peace and prosperity is God's desire for us. The Apostle John prayed for his friend Gaius *"that you may enjoy good health and that all may go well with you, even as your soul is getting along well."* (3 John 1:2 NIV) It is important to understand, though, that this

34

is not His central purpose for us. Paul says, that God "desires all men to be saved and to come to the knowledge of the truth." (1 Timothy 2:4) Health and wealth are not the standard for true spirituality. Health and wealth do not change the heart for the good. They do not change us into God's nature, and that is His ultimate purpose.

No Pain, No Gain

We know what this means in sports. Physical training requires real effort, and often, a good deal of discomfort. But there is a spiritual analogy as Paul shows us.

I do not run like a man running aimlessly; I do not fight like a man beating the air. No, I beat my body and make it my slave so that after I have preached to others, I myself will not be disqualified for the prize. 1 Corinthians 9:26-27 (NIV)

Paul knew well that, while the Gospel is the good news of the free gift of God in Christ, it does take a struggle to continue growing in the Christian life. He wrote to the Romans,

The Spirit Himself testifies with our spirit that we are children of God, and if children, heirs also, heirs of God and fellow heirs with Christ, if indeed we suffer with Him so that we may also be glorified with Him. For I consider that the sufferings of this present time are not worthy to be compared with the glory that is to be revealed to us.
Romans 8:16-18

We are heirs with Christ, sharing in His suffering. In II Corinthians 4 he calls these sufferings "our light and momentary troubles (that) are achieving for us an eternal glory that far outweighs them all..." (Verse

17). The Greek word for *troubles* means pressure. God applies pressure to our lives. Think of the example of a Dad teaching his child to ride a two-wheel bike. He steadies the child, perhaps holds on to the seat a bit, but then lets go and gives words of encouragement. The child may tip over, or get a bit frightened, but then Dad starts over again. The Dad is applying gentle pressure to get the child to learn.

We have often looked at Ephesians chapter 5 and its explanation of the relationship between husbands and wives. The passage ends in verse 31 saying that the marital relationship is a mysterious image of Christ and the Church. The importance in this passage for us right now is in verse 25 where husbands are told to love their wives as Christ also loved the Church and gave Himself up for her. This is speaking of a depth of love that is willing to give up life itself for the good of another, a true self-sacrificing love, what Scripture calls agape. This is the nature of God, and it is agape that he desires we exercise in all circumstances of our lives. This is not easy, since it is contrary to our fallen nature. It requires God's hand to bring it forth from us. This is where God uses the various trials of life to change our heart into his nature of agape love. Peace and prosperity do not teach us these lessons. It was Martin Luther who made the remark, "I consider my sufferings more necessary to me than my meat and drink."[3] For it was only through these that he drew truly close to God. God uses pain in our lives, in one form or another, to change us, and bring us to the place where we can love with his self-sacrificing agape love.

Having now been retired for a few years and reaching the age of 80 plus many changes have happened in my life, also in the lives of many of my contemporaries. Things I could previously do easily I can no longer do. I don't have full use of my left arm and having to be careful of my balance I'm barred from ladders. I don't have the endurance to serve my congregation as I did. What seemed to define my life no longer does. But beyond the things taken from me something more precious has been given. My closeness, worship, and dependance upon Jesus is so much more beautiful. The richness of faith and prayer have deepened. Further, what I've given up really doesn't matter to me that much any longer.

I heard the same thing in talking with a couple others in our congregation. Lives have been totally changed with former strengths no longer available for a woman who lost her husband after fifty-some years of marriage. Also, a very capable man who has been brought low by cancer and it's treatments. Both find their faith and strength in the Lord more precious. We have something now that is both beautiful and valuable. God has a way of giving beck something more valuable to those from whom something is taken when the focus changes from self to Jesus.

The Great Business of God's Life with Us is Teaching Us Agape Love

We have already spoken of the four kinds of love in the first chapter. Agape is God's love, total self-sacrificing love. It is suffering that produces a purer, loftier kind of love in us, God's love, and God's very nature. He is seeking to work his nature in us so that we can rule with him in eternity. There are no accidents for a child of God. All things are used in training for our relationship with Him. God chooses the tools. Have you ever watched someone working on a lathe? The wood is spinning at a high speed and the sharper the lathe tool, the finer, more perfect the result. God chooses the tools he needs. In John 15:1&2 Jesus tells us, *I am the true vine, and My Father is the vinedresser. Every branch in Me that does not bear fruit, He takes away; and every branch that bears fruit, He prunes it so that it may bear more fruit.*

I've always been fascinated by this verse. I can imagine what the branch feels like when it has the pruning shears come at it. God prunes His vines so that they bear more fruit. He cannot shape us without pain, but - and this is an important *but* - He never uses needless pain. Paul tells us, *No temptation has overtaken you but such as is common to man; and God is faithful who will not allow you be tempted beyond what you are able, but with the temptation will provide the way of escape also, so that you will be able to endure it.* (I Corinthians 10:13) We are not tempted beyond our strength. We hear people say, and we may have said ourselves, "Lord, I'm at my limit. I can't take any more." But God knows our hearts, and he does care deeply. He will not go beyond that which we can endure. We are true children of God. He is our Father. He loves us with an everlasting love, and He is doing his best to bring us into his kingdom.

It is not Easy in Our Fallen World. We are in a Spiritual Warfare.

We are redeemed, forgiven, and have a new life in Christ. Paul calls us a "new creation."(Galatians 6:15) But we still struggle with our fallen nature, as the Apostle clearly shows in Romans 7. Our inward nature is continually in the process of being changed, from one degree of glory to the next. (2Corinthinas 3:18) God works to change our fallen nature into Jesus' nature of agape. This is strongly opposed by Satan. Lucifer, is the fallen archangel who never understood the depth of that kind of love in God. Satan works to support our old nature in all of its prides and self-centeredness. At the cross, he is a defeated enemy, but he still prowls like a roaring lion trying to separate as many people from the grace of God as possible.(1Peter 5:18) When he gets us to yield to temptation, lift up our pride, display our anger unjustly, and harbor our resentments, he has defeated agape love in us and won a battle.

He has not won the war, and will not win the war, but he can degrade the image of God in us. We never have to yield to him. We do have the Holy Spirit working in our lives. We are taught that *the one who is in you is greater than the one who is in the world.* (1 John 4:4) NIV We are called to understand the work God is doing in us, and to yield to the Holy Spirit in all of our encounters of life. We will try to see more specifically how this happens as we continue our next chapters.

This Thing Is From Me

I want to share a writing with you by Laura Snow. She is commenting on I Kings 12:24 where the kingdom of Israel had been split in two. Judah, the southern part of the kingdom was about to go to war with the northern part, Israel. God tells the king not to do this because He has allowed the split to occur. While not His perfect will, He will seek to use it for the good of both parts of the kingdom. Snow writes:

My Child, I have a message for you today; let me whisper it in your ear, that it may gild with glory any storm clouds which may arise, and smooth the rough places upon which you may have to tread. It is short--only five words--but let them sink into your inmost soul; use them as a pillow upon which to rest your weary head: "THIS THING IS FROM ME."

Have you ever thought of it, that all that concerns you, concerns ME, too? for "He that toucheth you, toucheth the apple of His eye" (Zechariah 2:8). I would have you learn, when temptations assail you, and the "enemy comes in like a flood," that this thing is from Me: that your weakness needs My might, and your safety lies in letting Me fight for you. You are very "precious in My sight" (Isaiah 43:4). Therefore it is my special delight to educate you.

Are you in money difficulties? Is it hard to make both ends meet? This thing is from Me, for I am your purse-bearer, and would have you draw from and depend upon Me. My supplies are limitless (Philipians 4:19). I would have you prove my promises. Let it not be said of you, "In this thing ye did not believe the Lord your God" (Deuteronomy 1:32).

Are you in difficult circumstances, surrounded by people who do not understand you, who never consult your taste, who put you in the background? This thing is from Me. I am the God of circumstances. Thou camest not to thy place by accident: it is the very place God meant for thee. Have you not asked to be made humble? See, then, I have placed you in the very school where the lesson is taught; your surroundings and companions are only working out MY will.

Are you passing though a night of sorrow? This thing is from Me. I am the "Man of Sorrows, and acquainted with grief." I have let earthly comforts fail you, that turning to Me, you may obtain everlasting consolation (II Thessalonians 2:16,17). Has some friend disappointed you? One to whom you opened out your heart? This thing is from Me. I have allowed this disappointment to come, that you may learn that: "The best friend to have is Jesus. I want to be your confidant. Has someone repeated things about you that are untrue? Leave them to Me, and draw closer to Me, thy shelter out of reach of "the strife of tongues," for "I will bring forth thy righteousness as the light and thy judgment as the noonday." (Psalm 37:6).

Have your plans been upset? Are you bowed down and weary? This thing is from Me, You made your plans, then came asking me to bless them; but I would have you let Me plan for you, and then I take the responsibility; for "This thing is too heavy for thee, Thou art not able to perform it thyself alone." (Exodus18:18). You are only an instrument, not an agent.

Have you longed to do some great work for Me, and instead been laid aside on a bed of pain and weakness? This thing is from Me. I could not get your attention in your busy days, and I want to teach you some of My deepest lessons. "They also serve who only stand

and wait." Some of My greatest workers are those shut out from active service that they may learn to wield the weapon of all prayer.

Are you suddenly called upon to occupy a difficult and responsible position? Launch out on Me. I am trusting you with "the possession of difficulties," and for "This thing the Lord thy God shall bless thee in all thy works and in all thou puttest thy hands unto" (Deuteronomy 15:10).

This day I place in your hands this pot of holy oil; make use of it freely, my child. Let every circumstance as it arises, every word that pains you, every interruption that would make you impatient, every revelation of your own weakness, be anointed with it! Remember, "interruptions are divine instructions." The sting will go as you learn to see Me in all things. Therefore "Set your hearts unto all the words which I testify among you this day, for it is not a vain thing for you; because it is your life, and through 'this thing' ye shall prolong your days in the land" (Deuteronomy 32:46,47).[4]

While I think this is a very helpful writing giving us a lot to ponder, it should be noted that some circumstances are the consequences of our wrong choices. We cannot say that God caused us to make those wrong choices, or blame God for ever circumstance. Nevertheless, we realize that the grace of God is so wide that He never abandons us. He uses all things, even our wrong choices, to turn us to Him.

We Remember Our Calling to Reign WithChrist.

No other answer makes sense for a Christian. Why did this thing happen? We are never sure of a clear answer while we are in the midst of a circumstance. But we know that God is faithful. We are being prepared as a bride for our heavenly role in God's eternal kingdom. Speaking about all of the Old Testament faithful, Hebrews 11:13 tells us, "All these died in faith, without receiving the promises, but having seen them and having welcomed them from a distance, and having confessed that they were strangers and exiles on the earth". As nice as God has allowed us to have things in our earthly life, this is still not our permanent home. We are *strangers and exiles* in the earth. Jesus said, "In My Father's house are many dwelling places; if it were not so, I would have told you; for I go to prepare a place for you. If I go and prepare a place for you, I will come again and receive you to Myself, that where I am, there you may be also." (John 14:2-3) This thing is from Me. It will be for your great blessing.

> Beloved, do not be surprised at the fiery ordeal among you, which comes upon you for your testing, as though some strange thing were happening to you; but to the degree that you share the sufferings of Christ, keep on rejoicing, so that also at the revelation of His glory you may rejoice with exultation. If you are reviled for the name of Christ, you are blessed, because the Spirit of glory and of God rests on you.
>
> (1 Peter 4:12-14)

> After you have suffered for a little while, the God of all grace, who called you to His eternal glory in Christ, will Himself perfect, confirm, strengthen and establish you.
>
> (1 Peter 5:10)

> Therefore, we ourselves speak proudly of you among the churches of God for your perseverance and faith in the midst of all your persecutions and afflictions which you endure. This is a plain indication of God's righteous judgment so that you will be considered worthy of the kingdom of God, for which indeed you are suffering.
>
> (2 Thessolonians 1:4-5)

For to you it has been granted for Christ's sake, not only to believe in Him, but also to suffer for His sake...

(Philippians 1:20)

All of these texts emphasize the believers calling to suffer with the Lord Jesus Christ. Quoting again from Paul Billheimer, "There is simply no way to explain Biblical teaching on the glory of suffering and tribulation, except as an apprenticeship for the throne."[5] It is easy for us to doubt how our present situation fits into God's plan, and most likely we won't see it until some time after. But our trust is continually in the One who loves us, and who wants us to reign with Him. We are being trained for rulership. To rule with Christ, we must be of the same nature with Christ. That nature is agape. We can only learn agape through suffering, and that training is done now in our time on this earth.

We must also realize that the training God works in our life provides beneficial loving service to those around us in this present world. This is the reflection of Jesus' love that we seek to live as a daily witness whether at home, at our occupation, or at the shopping center. Our Lord's love and care matures us for all life, now and forever.

Notes

1   Lutheran Service Book, (St. Louis, Concordia Publishing House, 2006) 151

2   Paul E. Billheimer Don't Waste Your Sorrows (Fort Washington, PA. Christian Literature Crusade, 1977) 27

3   Martin Luther, The Table Talk, trans. William Hazlett, (Philadelphia, The Lutheran Publication Society,

4   Laura Barton Snow, "This Thing is From Me", Midnight Cry Messenger, January-February 1981

5   Ibid. Billheimer, page 81

CHAPTER 5

With Eyes Focused on Jesus

Thinking Beyond Salvation

Let me say from the beginning, we never get beyond salvation. The salvation work of Jesus Christ was an awesome sacrifice of the grace of God for mankind. When we get to heaven, and meet Jesus, He will still have the marks of the nails in His hands and feet. However, the way the word "salvation" is used in Scripture points to an ongoing work. For example, in Philippians 2:12-13 we read, "So then, my beloved, just as you have always obeyed, not as in my presence only, but now much more in my absence, work out your salvation with fear and trembling; for it is God who is at work in you, both to will and to work for His good pleasure". Paul says that we are to *work out our salvation with fear and trembling.* This is an ongoing action in each of our lives. It does not mean that we are unsure of our eternal salvation. We know that is God's gracious gift to us in Jesus Christ. Further, we know that our salvation is not by works, "so that no one may boast." (Ephesians 2:9) But verse 10 of Ephesians, like verse 13 of Philippians says that we are God's workmanship, it is God who works in us, continuing to change us in this salvation work. This is an ongoing process, some would call it sanctification. It is God working in us to reverse the affects of the Fall. We don't really realize how deeply we have fallen, having inherited sin from the rebellion of our first parents. God has a lot of cleaning up to do in us.

This does not happen automatically with our baptism, or even making a personal confession of faith in Jesus Christ. It is why Martin Luther taught that we are simultaneously saint and sinner. Let me give you an illustration. When we were in Florida some months after hurricane Katrina, our friends took us out on their pontoon boat. We rode up a barge canal. At one spot, there was a sunken houseboat on the side of the canal. In order to salvage the boat, it first had to be refloated, and the engine and mechanical structures repaired. The boat could now be operated again. It could move under its own power to a new birth. I compare this to salvation. The boat is up and working again, but there is a lot yet to do. Mud needs to be cleaned out. Badly damaged wood must be removed and replaced. Cleaning, painting, replacing furniture and a hundred other chores must be accomplished to restore the houseboat to its former livable condition. This is the ongoing work that God is doing in us. This really is a picture of us. You see, we can be saved and still have a temper; be saved and still harbor bitterness over long past events; be saved and be full of pride and arrogance. These things are not of God, and He desires to cleanse us completely. This is His ongoing work throughout life.

We saw how God uses pain, in one form or another, to get our attention and help us to yield that wrong part of our life to Him. His work is always for the purpose of preparing us for rulership in His eternal Kingdom. He is training a people for eternal service, and He can't use ones that still cling to things incompatible with His nature. We might also point out again, that this is the purpose of our time on earth, why we are here. No, we will not be fully complete when we die, but hopefully we have allowed God to make progress in us. Nor are we instantly perfect the moment we pass over to the other side of life. I have used words like *yield* and *allow*. This is to emphasize that it must be God's work in us by the presence of His Holy Spirit. He does the changing. However, He does not usurp our will. We can recognize what needs to be changed, and seek his grace to change it. Or we can resist his efforts every step of the way. We don't have to give up our bitterness, for example. We can resist his every effort to show us where we need to forgive and let go. But if we are willing, the cleansing power of the Holy Spirit will take the bitterness from us, and change our heart. We will be looking specifically at some situations in life that God uses to change us, and how we can respond and grow. But above all, we need to trust our Lord and be at peace.

Being at Peace

An underlying need for all of us is to be at peace in our hearts. This is the foundation on which our life is built. And that peace comes from our continual relationship with Christ. Isaiah 26:3 tells us, "You will keep him in perfect peace, whose mind is steadfast, because he trusts in You." (NIV) Peace does not mean the lack of difficulties or illness. We've already said that God uses these for our good. The peace that He speaks about here is a peace in the depth of our being because our trust is continually fixed on the Lord regardless of circumstances.

Jesus said to His disciples on that very stressful evening just before His crucifixion, "Peace I leave with you, My peace I give you; not as the world gives do I give to you. Do not let your heart be troubled, nor let it be fearful." (John 14:27) *Do not let your heart be troubled or afraid.* This is the peace that Jesus wants for us in all the circumstances of life.

We really don't know much about our own hearts. It is not just our mind, or our conscience. It is not synonymous with our soul. Our heart is the deepest part of our spiritual being, the part into which God breathed life at creation, and the part in which the Holy Spirit resides in the baptized believer. If the core of our being is at peace, then this radiates out to our mind and our actions. This is what Jesus was looking for in his disciples, for example, at the time they were all caught in the storm on the Sea of Galilee. Jesus was asleep in the back of the boat. The disciples cried out for help, and Jesus said, "Why are you afraid." (Matthew 8:26) I'm sure any of us would be afraid in similar circumstances, but He was looking for a new level of peace and trust in them. It is peace coming from our trust in Jesus that allows him to work changes in our hearts.

Two Scriptures from Paul
Philippians 4:4-7 and Colossians 3:12-17

We are learning in these chapters how to grow in agape love, God's sacrificial love for all people. That is to be the condition of our heart, and it must grow out of a heart at peace and complete trust in Jesus. Thus, the title of this chapter: *With Eyes Focused On Jesus*. Let's look at these passages to see what they say about peace and trust in our heart. I will put the two passages in chart form and then discuss them afterward.

Philippians 4	Colossians 3
Vs.4 Rejoice in the Lord always. I will say it again: Rejoice! **Learning to praise**	Vs.16 Let the word of Christ dwell in you richly as you teach and admonish one another with all wisdom, and as you sing psalms, hymns and spiritual songs with gratitude in your hearts to God
Vs.5a Let your gentleness be evident to all. **Living a life of meekness**	Vss.12-14 Therefore, as God's chosen people, holy and dearly loved, clothe yourselves with compassion, kindness, humility, gentleness and patience. Bear with each other and forgive whatever grievances you may have against one another. Forgive as the Lord forgave you. And over all these virtues put on love, which binds them all together in perfect unity
Vs.5b&6a The Lord is near. Do not be anxious about anything, **Depending on the Fellowship in time of anxiety**	Vs.15a Let the peace of Christ rule in your hearts, since as members of one body you were called to peace.

Vs.6b&7 but in everything, by prayer and petition, with thanksgiving, present your requests to God. And the peace of God, which transcends all understanding, will guard your hearts and your minds in Christ Jesus. **Praying with thanksgiving**	Vs.15b And be thankful
Vs.8 Finally, brothers, whatever is true, whatever is noble, whatever is right, whatever is pure, whatever is lovely, whatever is admirable—if anything is excellent or praiseworthy—think about such things. **Guarding your mind**	Vs.16a Let the word of Christ dwell in you richly
Vs.9a Whatever you have learned or received or heard from me, or seen in me—put it into practice. **Living as an example**	Vs.17 And whatever you do, whether in word or deed, do it all in the name of the Lord Jesus, giving thanks to God the Father through him.
Vs.9b And the God of peace will be with you. **Knowing God's peace**	Vs.15b as members of one body you were called to peace.

Learning to Praise

In Philippians 4:4 Paul tells us to rejoice in the Lord always. Praise should be our daily companion. This focuses our eyes on the Lord. Too often, when we are in the midst of difficulty, we can only see the problem, and our trust is weakened. We need to remind ourselves that God is always near. He cares about us in every situation of life. He doesn't automatically take away every hurt, but we are promised that He uses all things for the good of them who love Him and are called according to His purpose.[1] We have emphasized over and over that we are God's children for Jesus' sake. He has called us to the faith, and He has a purpose for our lives. We do not always or maybe more often than not, fully understand that purpose, but it is there, and praise focuses our eyes on Him in trust.

But how do we praise Him? A friend of mine, years ago, used to wonder about this. He would say, "After I've said 'praise the Lord' three times, what else do I say?" However, we have a wealth of words with which we can praise the Lord. Colossians tells us to use "psalms, hymns and spiritual songs." Scripture itself gives us many words we can take for our own.

> Psalm 148:1-5 "Praise the LORD! Praise the LORD from the heavens; Praise Him in the heights! Praise Him, all His angels; Praise Him, all His hosts! Praise Him, sun and moon; Praise Him, all stars of light! Praise Him, highest heavens, and the waters that are above the heavens! Let them praise the name of the LORD,"

> Psalm 33:1-4 "Sing for joy in the LORD, O you righteous ones; Praise is becoming to the upright. Give thanks to the LORD with the lyre; Sing praises to Him with a harp of ten strings. Sing to Him a new song; Play skillfully with a shout of joy. For the word of the LORD is upright, And all His work is done in faithfulness."

There are so many more. Then, there are the lyrics of our hymns written by faithful people over many centuries.

> *All Glory, Laud, and Honor* "All glory, laud and honor, To Thee, Redeemer, King, To Whom the lips of children Made sweet hosannas ring. Thou art the King of Israel, Thou

David's royal Son, Who in the Lord's Name comest, The King and Blessed One."[2]

A Mighty Fortress Is Our God "A mighty fortress is our God, a bulwark never failing; Our helper He, amid the flood of mortal ills prevailing: For still our ancient foe doth seek to work us woe; His craft and power are great, and, armed with cruel hate, On earth is not his equal. If we in our own strength confide, our striving would be losing; Were not the right Man on our side, the Man of God's own choosing: Dost ask who that may be? Christ Jesus, it is He; Lord Sabaoth, His Name, from age to age the same, And He must win the battle."[3]

Hymnody is rich with praise - *All Hail The Power Of Jesus Name*; *Rock of Ages;* or perhaps some of our Scriptural choruses - *Thou Art Worthy*; *Break Forth Into Joy O My Soul*, and others. Paul also mentions *spiritual songs*. This is singing with the word given by the Holy Spirit in a prayer language, or tongues as shown in I Cor.14:15. All of these provide us with an abundance of expressions that we can take for our own to use in praising our Lord, and thus keeping our focus on Him.

Living a Life of Meekness

In Philippians 4:5a Paul tells us to "let your gentle spirit be known to all men." And he explains this more fully in the Colossians passage. "Clothe yourselves with compassion, kindness, humility, gentleness and patience. Bear with each other and forgive whatever grievances you may have against one another. Forgive as the Lord forgave you. And over all these virtues put on love." (Verse 12) It is a fact that many people irritate us, or are dull, or overbearing, or have any number of attributes that can rub us wrong. They simply are not like us, rational and sensible as we are! But we have to deal with them. Some we naturally like more than others, but our opinion of them is really not the important thing. We are seeking to keep our eyes on Jesus, and learn to respond with His agape love. So we approach them with compassion, kindness, humility, gentleness and patience. We desire that others see Christ in us, not a short fuse of our own irritation. We are reminded to forgive as the Lord forgives us. Our model is our Lord on the cross. He forgave those who were still mocking and spitting on him. We are to look on each person as one for whom Christ died. This does not mean that we let people walk over us. We hold to our convictions. We "speak the truth in love."(Eph.4:15) Sometimes we must be hard on another person, but it is always done for their good. Jesus was frustrated and angry with people on a number of occasions, but it was never because He was personally attacked. It was because they offended His Father, like the money changers in the Temple,[4] or failed to understand the greatness of the gift He wanted to give them, as with Peter not accepting the truth of the necessity of His atoning death.[5] The essence of this life is in Colossians 3:14 "above all these virtues put on agape." This is what all of these chapters are about.

Depending on the Fellowship in Times of Anxiety

Philippians 5b&6a - "The Lord is near. Be anxious for nothing." I split the verses in this way because I believe these statements belong together. Scripture continually tells us not to worry, not to be anxious. In the Sermon on the Mount in Matthew 6:24 and the following verses, Jesus tells the people not to worry about their temporal needs. He says that God knows what we need and can provide it. Our job is to seek first the Kingdom of God and His righteousness. The problem is that, over the centuries, and especially in our modern time, we have complicated our lives with so many things, and so many different endeavors. We call it *life style*, and we have chosen a life style that causes us much worry and anxiety. We need to look at Paul's words to the Colossians. "Let the peace of Christ rule in your hearts, since as members of one body you were called to peace." (Verse 15a) In these passages of Scripture, we are emphasizing two things. First, that the Lord is near. And second, that we are members of one body. Jesus promised in Matthew 28:20 that He would be with us even to the close of the age. In Hebrews 13:5, we have His promise never to leave or forsake us. We must hold to these promises no matter what the circumstances in which we find ourselves. But, in fact, things do get very difficult at times, and we can't see the Lord clearly. That is why we are part of *one body*. We are not meant to carry burdens alone. We can call on the fellowship of believers. We have people that can pray for us and with us, who are willing to talk with and advise us, who are even willing to scrub our floors, if needed. We are a part of the Body of Christ, and that is a real strength. These are the provisions that our gracious Lord has given us to maintain our peace.

Making Our Petitions with Thanksgiving

Philippians 6b&7 - "In everything with prayer and petition with thanksgiving." We are a people of prayer. Christians are people in a relationship with their Saviour. The most natural thing in any relationship is to talk together. That's what prayer is. It is not just an exercise to sooth our minds. It is a two way communion with our Lord. We have said that He is near, and that He cares. He is our Bridegroom, which speaks of the intimacy of our relationship. Like any deep relationship, our communication is not limited to just our times of need. The old expression, "there are no atheists in a foxhole" does not apply here. It is why the expressions of praise with which we began this section are so important. We maintain a continuous relationship with our Lord.

But there are times of special need. We do take our petitions before the Lord. He has taught us to be persistent in our requests. "At all times we ought to pray and not lose heart." (Luke 18:1) According to verse 6 of Philippians our petition is made "with thanksgiving." This is an important qualification. We bring all of our prayers to the Lord, all of the requests and burdens of our heart, along with our thanksgiving knowing that He does hear and respond. Our thanksgiving, even when we have not yet seen an answer, is our act of faith and trust. It is the strength of our prayers. Paul added the words in Colossians 3:15 "and be thankful" emphasizing this point. It is out of the knowledge of our relationship with Christ, and our continual, thankful communication with Him that "the peace that transcends all understanding will guard our hearts."

Guarding Your Mind

Philippians 4:8 - After giving a list of virtuous things, Paul says, "think about such things." Another translation of the word *think* is *dwell*. Dwell on such things. To the Colossians Paul said, "let the words of Christ dwell in you richly." This is the old computer slogan, "garbage in garbage out." Or its converse for this purpose, "put good things in and get good things out." It is not a Pollyanna philosophy that ignores the bad things that happen around us. We are realistic in knowing the fallen nature of man, and see clearly the evils of our world. But these are not the things upon which we dwell. We do have many blessings to call to mind. However, even if we feel that there are few things we can call blessings, we can take up the expression of the Old Testament prophet Habakkuk.

> "Though the fig tree should not blossom, and there be no fruit on the vines, Though the yield of the olive should fail, and the fields produce no food, though the flock should be cut off from the fold, and there be no cattle in the stalls, Yet I will exult in the LORD, I will rejoice in the God of my salvation. The Lord GOD is my strength,"
>
> Habakkuk 3:17-19

We understand that this life is not all there is, and that we are strangers and sojourners upon the earth. Therefore, we do what we can where we can, but our hope is not in the conditions of the world, but in the amazing grace of our Lord. It is upon Him that we dwell.

There is a further truth that we need to consider with this verse. All sins start in the mind. What we let our mind dwell upon either controls our outlook, or shows itself out in our actions. Have you had those mental battles like I have at times? Someone has done something wrong, or offended us in some way. We play the whole thing over in our thoughts, *he said this, but I countered it this way. I showed him where he was wrong and took him down a peg.* Of course, we always win these battles, but it does us absolutely no good, and it only stirs up the animosity afresh. Our minds harbor thoughts of greed, pride, sexual lust, and more. All these are sins in the mind and keep our spirit and our whole life unsettled. Jesus was very clear that these sins are just as serious as sins acted out.[6] We cannot come to the peace that Christ desires if we continually let our minds dwell upon negative and sinful things. That is why the emphasis is upon dwelling upon the virtues of life.

Living As An Example

Philippians 4:9a - In this part of the verse Paul sets himself up as an example. "Whatever you have learned or received or heard from me, or seen in me - put into practice." What a marvelous statement. How many of us would dare to say that? But we should. Especially parents before their children. This does not mean that we are perfect and without sin. It doesn't mean that we never make mistakes, make a fool out of ourselves, offend or hurt others. It does mean that when we do make mistakes, when we do sin, we are willing to humble ourselves and ask forgiveness, even if it is one of our children that we have offended. It does mean that we strive to live a Godly example. We try to live by Colossians 3:17, "doing all in the name of the Lord Jesus." We put into practice all that we say we believe, and this becomes a powerful witness in the conduct of our life.

Knowing God's Peace

Philippians 4:9b - Paul summarizes the result of the life he has outlined in these verses, "the God of peace will be with you." As members of Christ's body we are called to peace, as in Colossians 3:15b. Remember Jesus' words at the Last Supper, "peace I leave with you..."[7] This is where we are to live in the depth of our heart. This is not freedom from distress, but a quiet trust in the depth of our being in all circumstances. The more our eyes are focused upon Jesus, making a practice of these six things in the Philippians and Colossian verses, the more the seventh, God's peace, will be experienced in our heart. This, then, becomes the ground out of which we can grow in the agape love of our Lord.

Notes

[1] Romans 8:28

[2] Theodolf of Orleans, 762 - 861, translated by John Mason Neale

[3] Martin Luther, 1483 - 1546

[4] John 2:14f

[5] Matthew 16:23

[6] Matthew 5:21 and following verses

[7] John 14:27

CHAPTER 6

Life Isn't Fair

Maturity

In our task of learning to live by God's agape love, we have an apprenticeship in this world and not in heaven. In the remainder of the text, I will call specific situations and times of life as "Life's Laboratories." There will be learning and growth in heaven. It is by no means a static place. It is occupied by all the saints who have gone before us, from whom we can learn much. We will be surrounded by agape in God's Kingdom, with infinite possibilities for learning and growth. However, it is here on this earth, seeing through a glass dimly, and having to walk by faith, that we are to be molded into God's nature of agape. And it is here that God uses our hardships to help us see and change.

We understand the outcome of this training in the natural realm of our families. Consider a child that is given everything it wants as it is growing up, with no chores or responsibilities expected of it, versus a child who learned that the family needed to be frugal, and who had their share of responsibility for the well being of that family. The one will grow up self-centered, and expecting the world to continue to provide. The other will carry its responsibility into adult life, and likely be successful. This is what growing into maturity is all about. Both children were born into the blessings of a family, but had to learn, or not, the maturity that is to come with growth. So it is with ourselves and our Lord. Our righteousness is a free gift of God's grace in Jesus Christ, but maturity as Christians must be learned as we grow in years and in the faith.

Webster defines maturity as being ripe or ready; having completed natural growth; having attained the desired state. This is a good definition of what God is looking for in us, *to attain the desired state of completed growth.*

Christian Maturity Is Not Primarily About Morality

Morality is really a side issue. For a Christian who understands the basics of Scripture such as the Ten Commandments, The Two Great Commandments, The Golden Rule, and The Sermon On the Mount, living a moral life should be a given. This is why those people who desire to get back to the ethos of the 1950s, or to the Reagan era, are really not providing a solution to our problems at all. James Dobson and the former Moral Majority lobbying Congress for new laws will not accomplish the maturity that God desires. True, it would be a more pleasant world to live in, and it should be the way people live and treat each other, but that is not all God is seeking. What God desires is always a heart that has been deeply touched and changed by Him, a heart that loves and wants more of God's nature. C. S. Lewis put it this way:

> People often think of Christian morality as a kind of bargain in which God says, 'If you keep a lot of rules I'll reward you, and if you don't I'll do the other thing.' I do not think that is the best way of looking at it. I would much rather say that every time you make a choice you are turning the central part of you, the part of you that chooses, into something a little different from what it was before. And taking your life as a whole, with all your innumerable choices, all your life long you are slowly turning this central thing either into a heavenly creature or into a hellish creature: either into a creature that is in harmony with God, and with other creatures, and with itself, or else into one that is in a state of war and hatred with God, and with its fellow creatures, and with itself. To be the one kind of creature is heaven: that is, it is joy and peace and knowledge and power. To be the other means madness, horror,

idiocy, rage, impotence, and eternal loneliness. Each of us at each moment is progressing to the one state or the other.[1]

C.S. Lewis, *Mere Christianity*

Every time you make a choice you are turning the central part of you (the heart, the dwelling place of God's Spirit) the part of you that chooses, into something a little different from what it was before. By our choices we are slowly turning the central part of us either into a heavenly creature or a hellish creature. And those choices are not primarily whether we return the extra change to the merchant, or not drink to excess. They are more about wanting to do those things that help us conform to the nature of God, like forgiving 70X7, holding our tongue, praying for an enemy, and sacrificing one's life, in whatever form, for the good of another. The moral life will naturally follow.

We Have Only One Right

Americans are steeped in the belief that they have rights. This is proclaimed in our Declaration of Independence - the right to life, liberty, and the pursuit of happiness; and in the Bill of Rights in our Constitution - religion, press, free assembly, bear arms, etc. We all enjoy these freedoms in our country. We look at other, particularly repressive regimes, and desire that they have these rights as well. Scripture teaches us that we are to work for justice and the good of others. Showing God's love in our lives does mean doing all we can for the good of others, but this does not mean that we expect or demand rights for ourselves. What we receive is in the hands of our gracious Lord.

The concept of human rights is not found in Scripture. God does want us to prosper and be in health as John points out in his third letter, but this is not our right. What we have is by pure grace, not by right. The concept of *rights* can lead us astray in our thinking about God.

The concept of rights puts man at the center instead of God, and it is exactly this that needs to change. It has been said that we have only one right, and that is to give up our rights. That is, to turn ourselves over in complete trust to the hands of God. This is the meaning of some of the hard sayings of Jesus. "He who has found his life will lose it, and he who has lost his life for My sake will find it." (Matthew 10:39) or "He who loves his life loses it, and he who hates his life in this world will keep it to life eternal." (John 12:25)

For us, life is not a question of fairness. In a fallen world, we should not look for or expect fairness. When we do receive it, it is grace with thanksgiving, but we are not crushed when we face the world's unfairness. That is its nature. We are not to expect fairness, but to trust ourselves completely to our God. This is the beginning of real maturity.

Our daughter Grace is 12 years younger than her sister Rebekah. Grace was in college at the time and the two of them were having a phone conversation. She was having a very stressful time with professors and with physical issues. She was sharing all of her stresses with her older sister. After a while Rebekah said, "that's what growing up is, kid." To which Grace responded, "growing up sucks!" Yes, it does. In the stresses of this fallen world, growing up is not always fun, but realizing this is where God can begin to use us. This is where He can begin to shape us into eternal people for His Kingdom. And that is a joy beyond anything this earth has to offer.

Making Choices

As cute as a baby can be, no one wants them to remain in that state. We are to grow in years and maturity. This is certainly true in our faith. Paul writes, "speaking the truth in love, we are to grow up in all aspects into Him who is the head, even Christ." (Ephesians 4:15) God does not force this on us. We have daily choices about how we respond to life's situations. This is what we see in the parables of Matthew 25. Each group of people represented, had a choice to make with what they were given. Did they take extra oil or not? Did they invest the master's money wisely, or did they bury it? Did they show compassion to people, or were they hard hearted? Their choices made a difference in the outcome of their lives. We have choices. How do we respond to life's situations?

We Must Be Decentralized

In order for God to use us, we must be changed from being self-centered to God-centered. I know I have used the terms fallen nature, and fallen world, a lot, but they must be central concepts in our understanding of our relationship with God. If we are not fallen, if we are not sinful by nature, then we don't need a Saviour, and all of the teachings of Scripture about redemption really have no meaning. But, in fact, we are fallen human beings. We have inherited sin from our first parents. We have accepted Satan's lie that "you surely will not die! ...you will be like God." (Genesis 3:4) One does not have to teach a baby how to be selfish. It is part of its nature. We all look out for "numero uno." From the time we are baptized into the faith, God begins working in us to help us be more God-centered than self-centered. As we shall see, the family is the natural place for this to begin.

Notes

1   C. S. Lewis, Mere Christianity, (New York, NY, Macmillian Publishing Co., 1952)

CHAPTER 7

Life's Laboratory # 1 The Family

The home is a complete laboratory for maturity with all of the stresses and strains under one roof. It was for Adam and Eve after they yielded to the devil's temptation. It continues to be so to this day. No two lives are in perfect harmony regardless of how well matched the couple was to begin with. It is a relationship of continuous learning. Each new period of life brings new lessons.

Most newly weds have not yet learned the meaning of unselfishness. This certainly was true for me. I'll give you an example of which I am ashamed that it ever happened, but it did. Audrey and I had been married a few months. She was working for a bank. I was home on a Saturday while she was at work. I wanted to make a sandwich, but there was no bread. I called her at work and complained, I'm afraid rather forcibly, about not having any bread. After all there was always bread in my mother's refrigerator. As I said, I am ashamed that I ever did that. We are now 57 years into our relationship the Lord has knocked some of my selfish edges off but I'm still a work in progress.

In the pre-marriage counseling I've done for couples, I used a personality and marriage survey. It examines a number of factors about each individual's background, personality, beliefs, and expectations. One of the measurements that I receive back is called their "idealistic distortion". That is, how much are they looking at this relationship through rose colored glasses. Usually, it is fairly high. They really don't yet realize the work they have ahead of them in becoming one flesh. These are not only secular couples, which I've seen most often, but Christians, committed to the Lord, yet still very much self-centered. God has a lot of work to do in us.

I have one shelf in my study that has nothing but marriage and family books on it, and this is only a small portion of those that have been published instructing people how to have a successful home life. It is not my purpose here to reiterate their advice, but to show that the stresses in marriage and family can go a long way in maturing us in Christian love.

And They Lived Happily Ever After! Really?

A good home and family is a place of peace and joy. It is my joy to be with my wife, children, and grandchildren. But marriage is not mainly about happiness. This is sometimes a shock to starry eyed couples, but it's true. Marriage is designed to decentralize the self. That is, to break through our natural self-centeredness. I tell couples that marriage is a 100% - 100% relationship, not the 50% - 50% that most think of. Couples with a 50% - 50% relationship can find ample reason to back out if they feel the partner isn't giving their fair share of effort. But a 100% - 100% relationship means that a couple is committed for life, and is willing to give of themselves completely to make the relationship work. To be sure it takes the commitment of both partners. It is why the marriage vows end with a promise, "till death we do part". A couple cannot enter into this depth of a relationship with an escape clause.

Stresses in the home are designed to produce brokenness, to move one away from self-centeredness to grace, sacrificial love, and gentleness. Paul speaks of the concerns in marriage to the Corinthians saying,

> One who is married is concerned about the things of the world, how he may please his wife, and his interests are divided. The woman who is unmarried, and the virgin, is concerned about the things of the Lord, that she may be holy both in body and spirit; but one who is married is concerned about the things of the world, how she may please her husband.

> 1 Corinthians 7:33-34

Paul is certainly not opposed to marriage, but he is being clear about the stresses that are involved. And for a Christian couple the desire to honor God with their new relationship. A couple will soon face differences in personality that they had not seen before, different patterns of communication, personal habits, sexual expectations, stresses in financial decisions, dealing with in-laws, differences in spiritual beliefs, different expectations in who will do what in the home, and all of this is before children come along. And living together before marriage is not the answer. Statistics prove that couples living together before marriage have a higher divorce rate than those who didn't.

The Bond of An Intiment Sexual Relationship

Learning the proper use and pleasure from an intiment sexual relationship has always been a challenge and a great source of temptation. Adolescence is the natural time when children becoming aware of sexual differences, attractions, and the feelings that go with it. Our twenty-first century world has greatly complicated proper growth to maturity as God intended. Smart-phones, the internet, the media, and peer pressure are confronting young people with information at earlier and earlier ages when they do not have the maturity to deal with it. The male and female genders are taught as having many variations. And where a natural male-female relationship begins to grow a sexual relationship before marriage is almost assumed. It's normal. It's fun. It's no big deal!

But in God's eyes it is a very big deal. The sexual relationship is God's gift to bind the man and woman together as one flesh, created in His image, with no shame for any past actions, a source of great pleasure, and personal holy fun. It is also intended for procreation. Children are a blessing. Oh, but this is another area where we want control over God. Our desire for career, home, and travel presented to us in our modern world along with the monetary cost to achieve them can make a pregnancy an impediment. So our medical knowledge and availability has given us alternatives.

I don't mean to come across in this text as judgmental and condemning. My wife and I have faced these same stresses. We've not always made right choices, but that doesn't change the standard by which God's people were created to live. God wants us to have the best life possible, but this can only come to fruition if we are willing to strive to follow His design.

Yes, This is the ideal

This is not an ideal that is impossible to reach. There are times when we've sinned before and outside of marriage. Times we let our feelings and emotions direct our decisions rather then seeking God to guide us. Times when our wants and desires ruled our lives. Jesus speaks of this in Matthew 19:8 as our "hardness of heart". This has caused us to sin rather than obey. This has caused times when divorce is a tragic necessity. These are not unforgivable sins, but they are not just an easy way out either. God can provide what is needed to obey His will. Divorce must be seen as a last resort after all means of reconciliation have failed. Our Lord can give a new beginning to a second marriage making it a beautiful image and maturing relationship. Our calling and challenge is always to seek God to rule our lives rather than the society around us. This has a cost, but the reward is more than worth it.

God created marriage in the first place. He made them male and female, and brought them together to be one flesh, one new person. This means that the old individual selves must die in order for the new person to come to life. And as many stresses as are laid on marriage because of our fallen nature and fallen world, God can make this new person, this union of two lives into one, truly beautiful. My wife and I are not perfect, but God has been working in us for fifty seven years, and we are that many times more in love now than when we began. But it takes work, and daily consideration for the needs of the other. Like all of the other situations of life, God uses these stresses to help us mature. If spouses can learn that neither marriage nor life is made primarily for personal happiness, then it is possible for growth to occur, and great blessings to be realized.

Jesus invites us to take up our cross and follow Him. That is, to willingly surrender our own prerogatives and accept the crucifixion of our pride for the good of another. Paul wrote, "I count all things to be loss in view of the surpassing value of knowing Christ Jesus my Lord, for whom I have suffered the loss of all things, and count them but rubbish so that I may gain Christ" (Philippians 3:8). To suffer the loss of all things includes our ego, our rights, and our sense of fairness, for the surpassing value of knowing Christ. Taking up our cross in this context does not mean we are weak, or that we do not stand up for right values, but it is getting ourselves out of the way so that we can show the nature of Christ's love and wisdom. The pressures of marriage, children, in-laws, and extended family all provide us with opportunities to move away from self-centeredness and grow toward maturity in Christ. The tragedy of broken homes, the demise of the nuclear family, and absentee fathers denies society of the place God intended to use for proper training.

Trouble in the Horizontal Means Trouble in the Vertical.

The Apostle Peter wrote, "You husbands in the same way, live with your wives in an understanding way, as with someone weaker, since she is a woman; and show her honor as a fellow heir of the grace of life, so that your prayers will not be hindered." (I Peter 3:7) Of course, there is always a disagreement about the wives being weaker, but that is not the point here. Peter is saying that we will block our own relationship with the Lord if we do not learn to honor our wives in a Christ-like way. In Ephesians 5:25 Paul has said that we are to love our wives "as Christ loved the church," that is sacrificially, and the wives are to respect their husbands. While these are lessons for both husband and wife, the primary responsibility for sacrificial love falls upon the husband. Then the wife's respect will flow more naturally. The Apostle John wrote,

> "Beloved, let us love one another, for love is from God; and everyone who loves is born of God and knows God. The one who does not love does not know God, for God is love...No one has seen God at any time; if we love one another, God abides in us, and His love is perfected in us...We love, because He first loved us. If someone says, 'I love God,' and hates his brother, he is a liar; for the one who does not love his brother whom he has seen, cannot love God whom he has not seen."

1 John 4:7-20

We can't say that we love God if we do not love (agape) our brother, or wife, or children, or any others God brings to us. Jesus also ties the vertical and horizontal relationships together in the Lord's Prayer - forgive us our sins as we forgive those who sin against us. There is a lot riding on our learning to live in God's sacrificial love, especially in marriage and family.

There are three priorities in life for married people: God first, family second and everything else third. Unfortunately, the stresses of modern life often place these priorities in reverse order, and for that we suffer. In a Christian marriage both partners must take seriously their own personal growth in Christ. They each need their own time for prayer and Scripture reading. This, too, takes discipline. Then they need to have time together in prayer and the Word.

The second priority is family. This means that time needs to be set aside for building relationships with spouse and children, even if it means giving up some good things like extra church functions or civic activities.

Some years ago a man paid me the highest complement I think I have ever had. He said, "If you do nothing else in your life you have raised five fine children". I've never forgotten that.

And then there is everything else, work, service projects, hobbies, whatever. This is where we have the most difficulty in organizing our priorities. According to a recent couples survey, "we spend an estimated 80 percent of our waking hours earning money, spending money, or thinking about money".[1] With such pressure it is no wonder that financial difficulties rank only behind adultery as the major cause of divorce. But with the Lord's guidance we can deal with this, and keep our priorities in order. Years ago a friend of ours gave up a good paying job and took his family back to the family farm so that he could be have a better life with them than they had in the stresses of urban life. Admittedly, this is an extreme move and not for everyone, but it does show that we can make some hard choices to do the things God desires of us.

Family life truly provides us with detailed laboratory work for learning to live and love in the Lord's nature. As God lives in us by the power of His Holy Spirit, His love is made complete. This is maturity and what God desires for each life.

Notes

1   David H. Olson, Amy Olson-Sigg, & Peter Larson, The Couple Checkup (Nashville: Thomas Nelson, 2008) 79-93

CHAPTER 8

Life's Laboratory #2 Unjust Suffering

What Happens To Us Is Not As Important
As Our Attitude Toward What Happens

The Apostle Paul writing to the Corinthian church says,

Therefore we do not lose heart, but though our outer man is decaying, yet our inner man is being renewed day by day. For momentary, light affliction is producing for us an eternal weight of glory far beyond all comparison, while we look not at the things which are seen, but at the things which are not seen; for the things which are seen are temporal, but the things which are not seen are eternal.

2 Corinthians 4:16 to 18

Paul's eyes were always on the goal "the upward call of God in Christ Jesus." (Philippians 3:14) Therefore he saw all of his many trials of life as aiming at that goal. He could call them "light, momentary affliction not worth comparing to the glory that would be revealed." Paul Billheimer writes, "One's afflictions can be made to work for him only by a correct subjective attitude." This is more than the power of positive thinking. It is keeping our eyes always on the true goal of life, and wanting to grow in the nature of Christ's love. Billheimer continued, "Nothing that comes to one from any source can injure him unless it causes him to have a wrong attitude. It is one's response that blesses or burns."[1]

I have visited many older people in nursing homes. I can't say this was always a pleasant experience. But there was one woman, the elder Mrs. Reed, whom I visited many times. In stages, she went from her home to the hospital, to an elder care facility. I know she was not happy about here failing health, her inability to be in her home, or being able to get around as she would like. Nonetheless, Mrs. Reed was a joy to visit. She blessed me in our conversations and times of prayer more than I to her. Her faith was strong regardless of her situation.

Consider Paul and Silas. They had caused a stir in Philippi and were thrown into prison.

> "When they had struck them with many blows, they threw them into prison, commanding the jailer to guard them securely; and he, having received such a command, threw them into the inner prison and fastened their feet in the stocks. But about midnight Paul and Silas were praying and singing hymns of praise to God, and the prisoners were listening to them;"

Acts 16:23-25

Their charge was unjust. They were beaten without a trial. They were put in stocks in the inner prison Yet, at midnight, in the dampness and dark of the cell they were praying and singing hymns. Their response led to the conversion of the jailer and his whole household. Their attitude was one of faith and trust, knowing that regardless of the outcome of this present trial, God was in control and they could rejoice even through pain.

Many Circumstances Are Beyond Our Control

We don't have a handle on all events, and, as we have all learned, unexpected things come frequently, sometimes in bunches. But with God's help we can control our reactions. How do we respond - with frustration, self pity, anger, rebellion toward God, or with patience, reason, and looking to the Lord for guidance? James writes,

Consider it all joy, my brethren, when you encounter various trials, knowing that the testing of your faith produces endurance. And let endurance have its perfect result, so that you may be perfect and complete, lacking in nothing.

James 1:2-4

"Consider it all joy" - not an easy thing to do. This is where we must have the Holy Spirit working in us. We cannot do this in our own nature. It is only through prayer and yielding to God that the right responses begin to grow. Paul shares the same thought in Romans 5,

We also exult in our tribulations, knowing that tribulation brings about perseverance; and perseverance, proven character; and proven character, hope; and hope does not disappoint, because the love of God has been poured out within our hearts through the Holy Spirit who was given to us.

Romans 5:3-5

Observe the list of characteristics that are produced in both of these passages. The ultimate result in rejoicing in tribulation is agape love, and this is supreme gain. Revelation 3:18 calls this "gold refined by fire."

A story is told of an elderly woman in London during the blitz of World War II. Bombs were falling and buildings were being destroyed. She was a woman of prayer, but her request was not to kill Germans and even to stop the bombings. Her prayer was very simple. "Lord, help me behave." She was asking for God's wisdom to know how to respond in whatever situation came her way. I have always thought this to be a marvelous prayer.

Wrongful Suffering

We do suffer unjustly, from harsh comments and accusations, to a variety of other things, many of which we did not cause. Our natural reaction, before suffering has done its work in us, is to be hard, harsh, arrogant, cutting, overbearing, tactless, or impatient. In other words, to fight back. We can run roughshod over another's feelings, sensibilities, and opinions. All of these traits are self-centered, which God wants to overcome in us. In the Galatian letter we read,

> For you were called to freedom, brethren; only do not turn your freedom into an opportunity for the flesh, but through love serve one another. For the whole Law is fulfilled in one word, in the statement, "you shall love your neighbor as yourself.
>
> Galatians 5:13-15

We are called to love, not to bite and devour. We need to allow God to get self (pride, ego) out of the way. Jesus was angry and frustrated on a number of occasions, but it was never because He was personally attacked. It was because His Father was blasphemed, or the values of God were rejected. He did not speak out of personal offense. This is why He could teach us to "love our enemy." God uses personality clashes, hostility, unjust criticism, and so forth as training for our response of love.

This does not mean that we don't speak our mind, or that we let wrongs go unanswered. Jesus had very harsh words for the spiritual deadness of the Pharisees. Those who felt His scourge as He drove the sellers out of the Temple knew His anger. But it was not because His pride was hurt or He felt He was treated unfairly. This is a hard and important lesson for us to learn.

Let's Add A Few More Related Scriptures

For to you it has been granted for Christ's sake, not only to believe in Him, but also to suffer for His sake,"

Philippians 1:20

Blessed be the God and Father of our Lord Jesus Christ, who according to His great mercy has caused us to be born again to a living hope through the resurrection of Jesus Christ from the dead, to obtain an inheritance which is imperishable and undefiled and will not fade away, reserved in heaven for you, who are protected by the power of God through faith for a salvation ready to be revealed in the last time. In this you greatly rejoice, even though now for a little while, if necessary, you have been distressed by various trials, so that the proof of your faith, being more precious than gold which is perishable, even though tested by fire, may be found to result in praise and glory and honor at the revelation of Jesus Christ;

1 Peter 1:3-7

For this finds favor, if for the sake of conscience toward God a person bears up under sorrows when suffering unjustly. For what credit is there if, when you sin and are harshly treated, you endure it with patience? But if when you do what is right and suffer for it you patiently endure it, this finds favor with God.

1 Peter 2:19-21

In each of these, and many more, suffering is connected to the glory that will be revealed. That glory is a life of servant love in

God's eternal Kingdom. We cannot yet imagine the depth of beauty, goodness, joy, fellowship, and even good holy fun that that will be. What we might have to face in this life is "not worth comparing" to the joy that is ahead.

Yes, it is hard not to feel resentment, or become cynical or bitter at unjust suffering, but if we are willing to take it to God, and get His help for our response, then we can grow in His deepest grace.

Notes

1   Paul E. Billheimer, *Don't Waste Your Sorrows*, (Fort Washington, PA, Christian Literature Crusade, 1977) 100

CHAPTER 9

Life's Laboratory #3 Physical Suffering

Where We Have Come Thus Far

Let me first recap a few important things we have established so far. We have said throughout, that we are here on earth being trained by God for His eternal purpose. We are to grow into the nature of Christ, and that nature is agape love. This self-sacrificing love is also represented by the fruit of God, the Holy Spirit, as shown in Galatians 5:22-23. "The fruit of the Spirit is love, joy, peace, patience, kindness, goodness, faithfulness, gentleness and self-control. Against such things there is no law." We have also said that this is beyond the basic understanding of our justification in Jesus Christ, that is, beyond basic salvation. It is a life-long growing process. We have our salvation by grace through faith in Jesus Christ. Nothing short of an outright rejection of Jesus Christ will cause us to lose our salvation. Now we are growing into maturity by the daily choices we make concerning the situations placed before us. Many of our choices are not easy, and we need Christ's guidance. We emphasized the need to focus our eyes upon Jesus, looking to Him in trust for all of our needs. In doing this, we have His peace, which is the ground out of which growth comes. Now we are looking at situations of life and how God can use them for our growth. We have looked at family life, and wrongful suffering. In this chapter we will be looking at physical illness. In the last chapters we will examine life's failures, and aging. We will see, I trust, how God works in each of "Life's Laboratories" for our good and for our growth.

Pain, Our Most Obvious Difficulty

We are all subject to the limitations of our physical body. We can't deny this, as Christian Scientists try to do. When something hurts, it hurts, and depending on the degree, it can consume our attention. This is true for everything from a cold to cancer.

We are to pray for healing. James tells us,

> Is any one of you in trouble? He should pray. Is anyone happy? Let him sing songs of praise. Is any one of you sick? He should call the elders of the church to pray over him and anoint him with oil in the name of the Lord. And the prayer offered in faith will make the sick person well; the Lord will raise him up. If he has sinned, he will be forgiven.
>
> James 5:13-15

We believe that prayer is effective. We have seen illnesses healed, or their duration shortened. God, our Father, invites us to bring all of our cares to Him.[1] However, not all are healed. When Paul was in Philippi his companion in ministry, Epaphroditus, was ill and nearly died. Paul said that God had mercy and spared him. At another time Paul wrote to Timothy with counsel about not drinking only water, but take a little wine "for the sake of your stomach and your frequent ailments." (1 Timothy 5:23) Both of these men had illnesses that were not healed, at least not immediately. A similar thing could be said of Paul's list of hardships he suffered.[2] At time make wrong choices against common sense and good medical advice. This leaves us open to pain and sickness. Other times pain is inflicted upon us by other, as with Paul.

We want to be clear in saying that illness and infirmity are not sent from God. They are not a punishment from God. God did use plagues against the Egyptians,[3] and once against the idolatrous king of Judah,

Jehoram,[4] but nowhere in the New Testament does God use sickness as a punishment. Rather, in more than one instance, it is attributed to Satan or a demonic spirit.[5] Certainly, not all sickness is from Satan, and we need to be careful not to see it that way, and we must not see it as punishment either.

Further, not being healed is not a sign of lack of faith. To believe this can also cause one to feel guilty and separated from God. While we are clear that illness is not sent from God, He is still in control, nonetheless. If he chooses not to remove it, He can still use it for our good. We will see more of this shortly.

We Live In a Fallen World

The Fall, the rebellion of our first parents, infected every part of creation, from the smallest atom, to the heart of man, to the cosmos itself. What this means in terms of physical difficulties is threefold.

1) We are subject to things that are not of our own doing. You are in a crowd where someone is coughing or sneezing. You get a cold. Elementary school teachers learn this quickly. Or far more serious is the spread of HIV. This is especially true in Africa. Many women have contracted the virus from a husband who, working away from home, visit prostitutes and brings it back with him. The mothers, in turn, pass it on to their unborn child. Sometimes things come to us through no fault of our own. Or perhaps, simply because we are getting older and our body is not as resilient as it once was.

2) We are subject to sins that are generations deep. They are a part of the lifestyle we have inherited and now choose to live. There are certain areas of the world, for example, where cancer is not as prevalent as it is in our country. People live a different lifestyle, with a different diet. There are stress related diseases, environment related diseases, and so forth.

Because we have wanted and created the modern, technological world we live in, we also inherit the ills that come with it.

3) Some physical problems do come from our own carelessness. Like falling off of a ladder! With some, the problem is self inflicted, as with drugs or alcohol.

Physical illness or pain is not God's best will for us as a means of training. There was no illness in the Garden, yet God began training Adam and Eve even before their rebellion. God would always rather that we learn of His nature without our suffering. He said to Israel through Moses,

> If you listen carefully to the voice of the LORD your God and do what is right in his eyes, if you pay attention to his commands and keep all his decrees, I will not bring on you any of the diseases I brought on the Egyptians, for I am the LORD, who heals you.
>
> Exodus 15:26

However, in our fallen state, God must often use our physical discomfort to get our attention, and to focus upon Him for our help.

However physical pain comes to us, it is still covered by Romans 8:28. "We know that God causes all things to work together for good to those who love God, to those who are called according to His purpose." God is still present. He is still our Father. He still loves us deeply and seeks the best for us. He is still using all things for our training and growth in Him.

The Question Is, How Do We Respond?

As with the previous chapter on unjust suffering, the question is not the condition itself, but our response to the condition. With an illness we certainly respond by availing ourselves of reasonable medical care. God has granted us much knowledge about diseases and their cure. We do not disdain this gift, and do seek treatment when it is needed. My emphasis here is on the word *reasonable*. There is certainly a difference between life-threatening and non life-threatening illnesses. But in any event, we are to use reasonable judgment, and the best counsel, in how far we choose to submit to treatment.

I'm reminded of the woman who came to Jesus for healing after suffering at the hands of many doctors for twelve years.[6] I certainly do not mean to degrade the medical profession. My point is that ultimately the choice of care must be in our hands.

We had a letter recently from a dear 89 year old woman in our church body who is suffering from lung problems. The doctor wanted to operate using a new procedure that may extend her life a few months or years. I must ask why, just as she did. Believing as we do, about our eternal life, why would we want to cling to every ounce of physical life, especially in an incapacitated state?

My mom had liver cancer. She chose not to follow any course of treatment except for pain medication. This was the right decision for her. It was a blessing to have her with us in our home for her last days on earth. One of our members and close friends was with her when she left to be with Jesus. Of course there is sadness and tears, but "we do not grieve as those who have no hope." (1 Thessolonians 4:13-14) For we are assured that, because of our faith in Jesus Chris, the best is yet to come.

Where a condition is non life-threatening we do all that is reasonable, but, in either case, the choices must be prayerfully our own. And our firm conviction is that all beyond this life is beautiful and good for those whose life is in Jesus.

The Physical Body Is Important

We do not take the Greek philosophical position that the spirit is good and the flesh is evil. The body was important enough for God to create it, and to inhabit it Himself for thirty-three years. We treat it as a gift from God. As with all His gifts, it requires our proper stewardship, meaning proper care, exercise, eating right, and not intentionally doing things to abuse it. We do all that is necessary and reasonable.

What we choose to do should be in the context of our trust and our peace with the Lord, as we discussed before. The reason that so many people, particularly the very elderly, cling to every ounce of physical life, is because of unbelief. For too many people, their belief in the goodness of God and His care in eternity is only a hope so and not a know so. Shakespeare expressed this in his character, Hamlet, who was contemplating his own end. We put up with a weary life because of "the dread of something after death, the undiscovered country from whose boundary no traveler returns."[7] For Christians this must never be an undiscovered country. We live in the firm belief that, because Jesus Christ was "raised from the dead through the glory of the Father, we too might walk in newness of life." (Romans 6:4) All of the truths of our faith must impact the decisions about our physical body.

Paul's Thorn in the Flesh
2 Corinthians 12:7-10

In the verses preceding this section, Paul has said that he had been caught up in the third heaven and experienced things so wonderful they could not be put into words. Now he finds himself with this infirmity which must have been sufficiently serious that he pleaded with the Lord to remove it. However, the Lord did not. But what Paul learned is very instructive for us.

To keep me from becoming conceited because of these surpassingly great revelations, there was given me a thorn in my flesh, a messenger of Satan, to torment me. 2 Corinthians 12:7 (NIV)

He is clear in saying that the infirmity is from Satan. It is not from God. It is a result of the Fall as we have already said. However, it is still under God's control. We are reminded of the account of Job and the calamities he endured. They were instigated by Satan, but Satan could only go as far as God allowed, and no further. It was used for God's purpose. In Paul's case, he is clear about the reason that it was given to him - to keep him from becoming conceited, or proud, because of the abundance of revelations he had experienced. For most of us the reason is not so clear. We may not see it until years later, if at all. Not knowing the reason, however, does not prevent us from learning lessons from it.

Three times I pleaded with the Lord to take it away from me.

2 Corinthians 12:8

And we should plead with the Lord. We are His children. He is our Father. We have spoken of His care numerous times. God loves us more than we can imagine. We can plead with Him for all of our needs. This does two things. First, it lets God know that we are serious about this request. Have you watched a child go through a toy store with a parent? They want this item, but then they see something else and want that. God wants to know if this is really a central concern for us, or are we just going through the motions of prayer. Then second, as we plead with the Lord, we begin to understand a bit more clearly how God is using this need. Prayer often works on us as much as it comes to God's ears.

But he said to me, 'My grace is sufficient for you, for my power is made perfect in weakness.' Therefore I will boast all the more gladly about my weaknesses, so that Christ's power may rest on me."

2 Corinthians 12:9

God answered, No. He told Paul that His grace was sufficient for his need. *Grace* - This places us back in the position of trust and peace that we have spoken about. There is an image out of the Book of Revelation, chapter six, verses nine to eleven where some of God's saints are crying out to the Lord to finish all of the suffering on the earth. They are given white robes and told to rest a little longer. God was assuring them that all things were in His control, and would be completed at the right time.

The First Lesson in the Laboratory of Physical Suffering is that we learn to rest in our Lord, to trust ourselves to His grace.

Further, God says, "my power is made perfect in weakness." This gives us a reason we can understand for our condition. It becomes a witness to others of how God's grace, God's power working within us, allows us to handle our condition. Remember my example of the elder Mrs. Reed. We spoke in the beginning of this chapter about the fruit of the Holy Spirit in Galatians 5. By God's power working within us, do we still display love, joy, peace, patience, and the rest of the fruit? Our illness or infirmity provides an opportunity to grow in the fruit of God's Spirit.

The Second Lesson is learning to handle illness with God's grace and the fruit of the Spirit.

In sharing these things, I don't mean to put judgment on anyone. I am the first to admit that these are not easy lessons to learn. When I am sick or in pain, I can be quite grumpy, and show anything but the fruit of the Spirit. But I do recognize this as a problem I have, and not simply pass it off as being the natural response. Yes, it is the natural response, but we are called, and helped, to grow beyond our fallen nature.

Paul says that he will boast in his weakness, that the power of Christ may dwell in him. The word *boast* can also be translated *glory, joy,* or *rejoicing.* His eyes are on Jesus and he is thanking Him for the way He is using it in his life. We are reminded in Philippians 4:6 that we are to make our "supplication with thanksgiving." We lay all of our serious requests before our Father, along with thanking Him that He hears, cares, and will respond.

> That is why, for Christ's sake, I delight in weaknesses, in insults, in hardships, in persecutions, in difficulties. For when I am weak, then I am strong.
>
> 2 Corinthians 12:10

The word *delight* can also be translated *content,* or *to think well of, to approve.* Paul is satisfied knowing his suffering is being used for God's purpose. This is what he will later write to the Philippians, "Not that I speak from want, for I have learned to be content in whatever circumstances I am." (Philippians 4:11) To be content in whatever circumstance, not angry, irritated, or asking "Why me?", but willing to do what is necessary and reasonable, and trust God for the rest.

This, then, is the *Third Lesson* from Paul's words, the paradox of faith "when I am weak, then I am strong."

These three lessons: learning to rest in God; handling our difficulties with the fruit of God's Spirit; and in our weakness finding God's strength, all together provide a powerful witness to the grace of our Lord.

There is yet a *Fourth Lesson* we can take from an infirmity, especially one of long duration, It may be a change in direction for our life. It is one that we certainly did not plan, but that can bring glory to God. There is the wonderful account of Joni Erickson Tada. Many of us are familiar with her ministry. As a teen, Joni suffered a broken neck in a diving accident which left her a quadriplegic. It was not the life she had hoped for, and initially she went through anger and denial, until she came to a deeper faith in the Lord. Over the years Joni has developed an international ministry to the handicapped that has touched thousands of lives. God didn't cause the diving accident, but He certainly used it for Joni's good and His glory. Her life, and the lives of many others, has well proven the words of St. Paul.

I don't mean to make light of any suffering. All of the trials we go through in life, the challenges we have, the pains we suffer are hard. They hurt. They confuse. The seem to isolate us. We've previously read many of the passages I've used. We believe them, but now here we are challenged and hurting, seeking to figure out what I should say next, what do I do now. We are totally dependant upon God, the Holy Spirit. The more we grow and mature through Life's Laboratories the more we can live in the "peace of God that passes all understanding". (Philippians 4:7) And that is a blessing beyond all measure.

Notes

1   I Peter 5:7

2   II Corinthians 11:23f

3   Exodus 9:14

4   2 Chronicles 21:18

5   Luke 13:11, 2 Corinthians 12:17

6   Mark 5:26

7   William Shakespeare, soliloquy, *Hamlet Prince of Denmark*

CHAPTER 10

Life's Laboratory #4
Life's Failures

Cleaning Up the Heart

God sometimes uses life's failures to decentralize us. That is, to move us away from being self-centered to being God-centered, to overcome our natural selfishness. Sometimes the only way God can produce meekness, compassion, and selflessness in us is to allow us to fail at some important task of life. David had a great failure in his sin with Bathsheba recorded in 2 Samuel 11. He speaks of that sin in what we know as Psalm 51, and his expression is what God is looking for in one who realizes his sin and repents. In verse 17 he says, "The sacrifices of God are a broken spirit; A broken and a contrite heart, O God, You will not despise." A broken and contrite heart is one that focuses upon God for strength and help, not on self-justification, rationalization, finger-pointing or any other escape. The sinful heart must look to God alone for forgiveness and restoration.

Sin is a Mixture in Our Hearts

After speaking about matters of conscience, Paul makes the statement that "all that is not of faith is sin" (Romans 14:23). To the Church at Colossi Paul had written, "Whatever you do, whether in word or deed, do it all in the name of the Lord Jesus, giving thanks to God the Father through him" (Colossians 3:17). All from faith - all in the name of the Lord, a difficult standard to follow, and, in fact, we know that we do not follow it well. We are, at the same time, saint and sinner. This is the mixture that exists in our life. It was Paul's struggle that he expresses in Romans 7:19 when he says, "the good that I want, I do not do, but I practice the very evil that I do not want." This could leave us despairing if it were not for the great grace we have found in Jesus Christ. Paul concludes this lament with a declaration of victory. "Thanks be to God through Jesus Christ our Lord!...there is now no condemnation for those who are in Christ Jesus." (Romans 7:25 and 8:1) We are a mixture, but by God's grace in Jesus Christ, we are not condemned. God is with us, and seeks to work with us each day to cleanse our heart and remove more of the mixture from us.

Removing Mixed Motives

God allows failure to purify motives and to remove mixture. God cannot abide mixture. This was the constant lesson for the Hebrew people. All of the laws and instructions from God were to reinforce the truth of the first commandment.

> You shall have no other gods before Me. You shall not make for yourself an idol, or any likeness of what is in heaven above or on the earth beneath or in the water under the earth. You shall not worship them or serve them; for I, the LORD your God, am a jealous God.
>
> Exodus 20:3-5

As an example, we can think of jealousy in the context of the marriage relationship. While a husband and wife are to feel secure with each other, we know what happens if one partner is unfaithful to the other. This causes great pain, and destroys the once strong trust. The unfaithful spouse has mixed or divided his loyalty. This mixture is extremely damaging. The same is true in our relationship with our Lord, our spiritual husband.

God declared through Isaiah that "My glory I will not give to another" (Isaiah 48:11). It is certainly not that God is an egomaniac, or a tyrant demanding allegiance. He is a God of love who cares deeply for His creation. He knows that the very best for His creation can only be found in harmony with Him, and not in harmony with Him plus something else. Harmony with God cannot be found in mixture. God showed this to Israel in His command not to intermarry with foreign peoples, or even, as an illustration, not to wear garments made from two different kinds of thread. We may not care about mixing two kinds of thread in the same garment. We do this all the time. Christ has freed us from the Old Testament legal code. But our mixtures, our divided loyalties, are far more serious. We let the demands of the lifestyle we've chosen, pull us from our devotion and trust in the Lord. Pride and the desire for personal recognition become more important than humble, unsung service.

How many prominent preachers and ministries have we heard about in recent years that have failed because of gross sins? I believe, in each of these, there was a sincere desire to do the work of the Gospel, but people get caught up in the perks of success. Being in the spotlight is difficult for anyone to handle, and to still remain true to the simple mission of their calling. In the previous chapter we heard Paul say that his "thorn in the flesh" was used to keep him from becoming conceited because of the many revelations God had given him. There is a great difference between zeal for God's Kingdom and ambition that gets mixed with personal pride. Temporal success is not always a measure of God's blessing, especially in the Church. There are times when God allows failure to purify our motives and to remove mixture from our life.

Upon What Do We Build?

Paul's words to the Corinthians are instructive for us.

According to the grace of God which was given to me, like a wise master builder I laid a foundation, and another is building on it. But each man must be careful how he builds on it. For no man can lay a foundation other than the one which is laid,

87

which is Jesus Christ. Now if any man builds on the foundation with gold, silver, precious stones, wood, hay, straw, each man's work will become evident; for the day will show it because it is to be revealed with fire, and the fire itself will test the quality of each man's work. If any man's work which he has built on it remains, he will receive a reward. If any man's work is burned up, he will suffer loss; but he himself will be saved, yet so as through fire.

Corinthians 3:10-15

The only true foundation for life, Jesus Christ. This means understanding and desiring to be like Jesus, to share His nature. What is it that we want in life? Are we striving for those things that help us become more like Jesus, and that will bring glory to God? We have choices about what we strive for. Those choices become the foundation upon which we build our life.

A man's foundation can be of gold, silver, precious stones, wood, hay, or stubble. These can be the qualities of meekness, compassion, selflessness, and so on, as we mentioned above. Or they can be prideful, self-serving and mixed with selfish aims. When our foundation, the times of our life, are tested by fire, it reveals what it is made of. We have seen or read of many natural disasters in recent years. A tornado will rip through a town destroying homes and businesses. This is a horrible occurrence. It would be a great tragedy for any of us. The question however is, what would it do to our hearts? What would it do to our trust in the Lord? In the midst of tragedy are we crushed and bitter, or are we thankful to be alive, and trusting God for the future? What is our foundation? In the letter to the Hebrews the writer, speaking of a time of Christian persecution, says of the people, "You accepted joyfully the seizure of your property, knowing that you have for yourselves a better possession and a lasting one." (Hebrews 10:34) I never mean to make light of any tragedy, and I know it is easy to write this when not confronted by the situation, but the point of the foundation upon which we build is still clear. We are to build upon those things that cannot be destroyed by any earthly condition.[1]

But even here, the God of all grace gives a promise. Even if all of one's earthly works are burned up, salvation is still possible. There will be many in heaven that will be saved, but will be far from the maturity God desires. God is always working with us in this life to purify our motives and remove our mixture. The choices are ours.

What Is True Success Before God?

So much of modern life is aimed at worldly success. We push our kid to achieve. We believe that college is essential for success. But why? If we understand the purpose that God has for us in this life, what are we striving to achieve? Now, understand that I am not opposed to a college education. All seven of us in our immediate family have a college degree. Education is important. God doesn't give any medals for being dull or lazy. In the world, we have the responsibility to support our family, and we want to choose a profession that we enjoy. All of this is fine and right, but it doesn't change the question about what we are working for in life. Compared to other industrialized nations, Americans are workaholics. We put in longer work weeks, and have less vacation time than many other countries. We are in an economy where both husband and wife need to work to maintain the lifestyle they desire, and children are in daycare. In the process, family time and quality are sacrificed. Let me share a little story that is humorous, yet biting with truth.

> A New York City businessman goes to Mexico. While wandering along the beach he sees a fisherman pulling his boat up onto the shore early in the day. The New Yorker says to the fisherman, "Hey, why are you stopping so early in the day?"

The fisherman says, "Well, I just did a little fishing and now I am going to play some music, play with my children, lay in the sun, and maybe later I will go out with my wife."

The businessman says, "Oh no, no, no! Take it from me, you should fish all day, then sell it to make more money."

"But why would I want to do that?" the fisherman asked.

"Then you could hire some helpers to work with you, and you can get a bigger boat later on. Once you do this, you will be making even more money, so then you can buy more boats and get more people to work for you."

But why would I want to do that?

"Then eventually you can move to New York and operate your business from there to sell your fish world-wide and make even more money!"

The fisherman says, "Why would I want to do that?"

The New Yorker says, "Because once you have a big company that sells its products world-wide, you can then sell your company and make millions! You could retire to a little beach town in Mexico and just relax, do a little fishing for yourself and your family, play with your children, play some music with your friends, and take your wife out at night whenever you feel like it!"

The fisherman just smiles at the New York businessman and walks away.

Being Christian, and beginning to understand the great purpose that God has for us in life, we always need to ask questions about our direction and what it is God would have us be doing. Should we or can we accept less in this world, even what looks like failure, and still fulfill the purpose for which God created us? The statement is true, with numerous examples of support, that one who gains the world's success without learning agape love has totally failed at life.[2]

Those Who Have Learned Through Failure

The Bible is full of examples of those who have failed, and yet God matured them and used them for great purposes.

- Joseph was a boastful kid who, because of his attitude, got himself sold into slavery, spent time in jail, and was finally elevated by God to a position where he could save his family.

- Moses had a stammering tongue, he resisted God, his anger kept him out of the Promised Land, yet he was a mighty deliverer for his people, and was called a friend of God.

- David we already spoke of concerning his great sins of adultery and murder, yet he is a man after God's own heart, and a fore bearer of the Christ.

- We could mention Jeremiah, Amos, Habakkuk, and all of the prophets, yet they were spokesmen for the Lord.

- We are aware of the numerous failures of the Apostle Peter. Because of his lack of faith he was almost drowned. His lack of understanding of the Lord's mission got him rebuked and called Satan. His boastful pride crushed him when he denied the Lord three times. But he was turned into a mighty Apostle who served the Lord well, even to martyrdom.

- Even our Lord, Himself, by worldly standards, was a failure. He ministered among the people for three years, spoke hard enough words that most of His followers left Him, and got himself in trouble with the authorities to the point of getting Himself killed. Yet, He is the Redeemer of mankind who has overcome the power of death for all time.

When we understand and accept the true purpose for which God has placed us on this earth, it changes our whole understanding of what is success and what is failure.

Life Is About Learning To Love

This is the theme of this whole text. Life is not about sensual pleasure, accumulating riches or fame, building great manufacturing empires, or having commercial, military, or political success. There are numerous examples of those reaching these goals yet leaving in their wake adultery, divorce, greed, deceit, and so forth. Billheimer has written, "If one has learned to love in this life he is a success no matter if he has failed otherwise."[3] The Apostle Paul long ago preceded Paul Billheimer with the same thought. "But now faith, hope, love, abide these three; but the greatest of these is love." (1 Corinthians 13:13) And Jesus, quoting from the Old Testament said,

You shall love the Lord your God with all your heart, and with all your soul, and with all your mind, and with all your strength. The second is this, you shall love your neighbor as yourself. There is no other commandment greater than these."

(Mark 12:30-31)

Not All Effort and No Joy

I know this sounds like a great challenge for all of us, and it is. But I don't want it to sound like it is all our work and there is no joy. We do have choices to make, but the work is God's within us. He is working to mold our hearts. Learning to love is learning to grow into God's nature. In this, we are growing closer to Him, which can only be pure joy. Our life is a balance that is expressed in Revelation 1:9, "I, John, your brother and fellow partaker in the tribulation and kingdom and perseverance which are in Jesus." We share in Jesus' *tribulation* because of the fallen nature of this world, the *kingdom* which is the knowledge of the joy that is always part of our Lord's life, and the *patient endurance* in the strength that God supplies.

Notes

1   See also Matthew 6:20, and Matthew 10:28

2   See Mark 8:36-38

3   Paul E. Billheimer, Don't Waste Your Sorrows, (Fort Washington, Pa, Christian Literature Crusade, 1977) 119

CHAPTER 11

Life's Laboratory #5
Learning Through Aging

Aging Is a Part of God's Design. It Comes To All of Us

Solomon, writing in Ecclesiastes describes the aging process in poetic fashion.

> Remember your Creator in the days of your youth, before the days of trouble come and the years approach when you will say, "I find no pleasure in them"- before the sun and the light and the moon and the stars grow dark, and the clouds return after the rain; when the keepers of the house tremble, and the strong men stoop, when the grinders cease because they are few, and those looking through the windows grow dim; when the doors to the street are closed and the sound of grinding fades; when men rise up at the sound of birds, but all their songs grow faint; when men are afraid of heights and of dangers in the streets; when the almond tree blossoms and the grasshopper drags himself along and desire no longer is stirred. Then man goes to his eternal home and mourners go about the streets. Remember him—before the silver cord is severed, or the golden bowl is broken; before the pitcher is shattered at the spring, or the wheel broken at the well, and the dust returns to the ground it came from, and the spirit returns to God who gave it.
>
> Ecclesiastes 12:1-7

Most consider aging anything but poetic. Yet it is a time of life that God can use to great advantage.

After the rebellion of man, the way was barred to the Tree of Life. [1] This way would not be opened again until the completion of all of God's plans. [2] God had a purpose for the long lives of the first generations. Adam died at 930 years. Abraham lived to be 175 years. Moses to 120 years, and the natural life span now according to Psalm 90:10 is 70 years, or if one is strong, 80 years. But death is inevitable for everyone, and the aging process constantly reminds us of this. The world wants to evade this at all cost. We have developed creams, potions, cosmetic surgery, and even lies to prolong the illusion of youth. It is natural to want to look our best whatever our age, but age is not to be denied, and for Christians, it can be embraced as a blessing.

There is a story I heard many years ago about a son who attended his father's funeral.

It was the standard funeral with which we are all familiar - visiting at the funeral home, the open casket for people to view the body, the offering of condolences to the family. Generally, the funeral director will have the family come in a hour before the visiting to say their good byes. On this occasion the son looked at his father's body in the casket and was upset with the work of the funeral director. As is usual, makeup had been applied to the face and hands, the hair had been colored slightly, and effort was made to hide the wrinkles. The son asked for a damp rag and began to wash away the director's work. He later explained that those wrinkles and gray hair were marks of his father's wisdom gained through many years. The son said that he, himself, had caused some of those marks of age with his wayward behavior. All of those were marks of his father's patience, forgiveness, and grace. They were marks of honor and should not be hidden.

I'm not sure that we would have the nerve to do as this son did, but the point is clear. Much is gained in age that cannot be learned any other way, and can be truly beautiful. No one likes the pains and limitations of age, but it has a purpose in God, and should be accepted gracefully.

The Revising Of Values

Age has its way of revising our system of values. We have a different set of priorities in older years than we did as a youth. When I was younger, I had multiple hobbies. I was into amateur radio, photography, model building, and carpentry. My wife loves to tell the story of how I rebuilt a chain saw in the small bathroom of our apartment. I had built a workbench over top of our bathtub. It was only a little awkward having to take a bath by crawling under the workbench. Oh, the patience of my dear wife! I collected radio parts, and drug boxes of paraphernalia from one move to another. Somehow, as I have gotten older, many of these things hold little further interest. I trust this is some growth.

Youth often think of themselves as deserving of all the benefits of life. Young people raised in our affluent society expect to begin their lives with the things that their parents took forty years to acquire. It takes time, and a few knocks, to learn that this is not true. Tragically, some in their thirties and forties have not learned it, expecting life to still provide them a living. God intends that the experiences of life, the disappointments, heartbreaks, financial struggles, ingratitude of loved ones, the grief of bereavements, and infirmities of years, change this attitude. The passing years with its joys and sorrows wean one away from self-worship. Aging, like the other struggles we have previously discussed, can help us move from being self-centered to being God-centered. However, getting older is not getting better unless it delivers one from self-love. It is intended to make one more gentle, thoughtful, considerate, gracious, sympathetic, and less childish and demanding. Like the other trials of life, we can yield to God's direction and seek to learn, or we can resist and grow sour. Hopefully, it can be the former.

God's Finishing School

Realizing our Age

Fruit takes time to ripen. Each of the seasons of life is used to ripen us into maturity. Each of the seasons is good, and each of life's experiences, down to old age, are working together to mature and ripen character and develop agape love. Aging is not just something to be endured as an unfortunate and unavoidable evil. It is part of God's plan. When properly accepted, it is God's finishing school for character education and enrichment before entering eternity.

I am writing this revised edition of my book fifteen years after the original. It is at a time when I've been through the challenges of retirement, health issues, and weakness. It is perhaps one of the hardest lessons I've had to learn. I've not done it all that well. Losing the ability to do, to serve, to go, to accomplish as I did just a few years earlier has been tough. I haven't gone into depression, but I've certainly had my times of feeling sorry for myself. Perhaps even making life a bit miserable for my family. I've just proved again that "I am by nature sinful and unclean" as we confess in each of our Sunday worship services. Apart from the redeeming grace of Jesus I really am a failure. Now, some four years into retirement, I have begun to see the value and joy our Lord provides in this stage of life. Ultimately a Christian never retires. They just change their mode of Christian service.

Retirement is not a Biblical concept. I know it is something that most people in industrialized societies plan for. Yet, it can be wasting years of life if not received properly. As we grow older, we do look for a time of less physical activity, and the stress of earning a living and raising a family. We do enjoy a time of not having to follow the clock as strictly. But this does not necessarily mean being unproductive. The great temptation is to follow the pattern of the world seeking one's own pleasures. Especially if we have extra funds, there is the opportunity to *do those things we always wanted to do*. This is the theme behind the movie, *The Bucket List,* two men seeking all of the thrills they wanted in life before they kick the bucket.

It is not wrong to use some of our leisure time and savings to travel or visit family and friends in distant places. My wife and I have had some wonderful trips, both in the U.S. and Europe. We've renewed friendships and the places we've seen have allowed us to have visible images and personal experiences with places we've only read about. However, if one is not able to realize these dreams, because of time, health or finances it should not be a source of frustration or feeling deprived. What we call the Retirement Years hold more value than completing a bucket list.

Using The Wisdom and Grace God Has Given

Spiritually our older years can be the most productive time of life. It can be true even if someone is physically limited. I've related previously in Chapter Four how having former strengths and abilities denied us because of age have caused some to draw nearer the grace and strength our God provides. We've learned the truth that what we've gained is more precious than anything we can no longer do. (Philippians 3:8) We can begin to realize that what is denied us in the aged weakness is more than given back in the beauty of a richer faith and fellowship with Jesus. I also told you about the elder Mrs. Reed who, though bedfast, was a joy to visit and was a blessing to those who came to serve her. These are not automatic blessings with age and not always easy to realize, but they can happen as we look to our Lord for the tasks He has for us in this time of life.

One of the great advantages of age, especially in this twenty-first century, is being able to have experienced societal changes over a long period of years. That does not mean a "longing for the good old days". Every age has done that, but we have seen changes come about more rapidly than ever before. These have been brought about by the devil's temptations moving the world further away from God and His love. The good old days were a bit slower paced but they really weren't all that good anyway.

Professor Peter Kreeft whom I referenced in the Introduction, is a professor of philosophy at Boston College and Kings College London. In the 1960 he taught a course on Aldous Huxley's 1932 book The Brave New World. It portrayed a futuristic world of human engineering whose fictional inhabitants apparently have a world full of love. Love, that is, where everyone is happy now. There is free sex with no social sanctions and no guilt; free drugs; and endless mindless entertainment, but no pain, no passion, no agony, no ecstasy.... In other words, Dr. Kreeft wrote, "life as it actually exists for the average American teenager in the 1990s." [3]

His course was intended to look at a dystopian world akin to George Orwell's 1984. Dr. Kreeft wrote that "The first time I taught the book was the occasion for a profound shock. I discovered the New Men: my students. (This was back in the sixties.) In discussing the book in class, it gradually dawned on me that many of my students were fundamentally misunderstanding it as a utopia instead of a dystopia, thinking Huxley was advocating it. Then came the second, deeper shock: they were all for it! They longed to live in Huxley's Brave New World.

"If a time machine could dip into the fifties and pluck out an uncle, an ordinary uncle, deposit him in the nineties and simply show him the empirical facts - MTV, Howard Stern, public high school sex educations classes - he would probably literally be unable to believe it."

In 1958 Huxley reviewed his previous work and said he was wrong about only one of his predictions: the timing. "It is coming much faster then he thought." Well we have been moved not by a time machine, but by our natural aging. We are now in the second decade of the third millennium. Consider the changes that we see today. Would we have believed it in the 1990s? How much further have we seen our world move from our Father's grace? What conditions do we see today that call for our earnest prayers? What influence can we still render to our own children, now parents themselves, and grandchildren? This calls us to some serious meditation; scripture reading; prayer; and sharing as our Lord leads.

Our elder years allow us time and perspective to see and understand more of what is happenings in the daily new reports. Prayer, particularly, is of great value. This may seem simplistic, and not really being *active*. However, prayer is the most powerful ministry and service to others anyone can have. Jesus expressed the importance of prayer, "telling them a parable to show that at all times they ought to pray and not to lose heart." (Luke 18:1) Jesus, Himself, depended upon prayer, and said that "the Son can do nothing of Himself, unless it is something He sees the Father doing..." (John 5:19) Prayer was the undergirding for Jesus' ministry.

The retired and the elderly Christians should be one of the greatest force available to God. Satan's most successful strategy is to keep Christians busy with secondary things, and away from prayer. We must be reminded that we are in a spiritual warfare.

> Be of sober spirit, be on the alert. Your adversary, the devil, prowls around like a roaring lion, seeking someone to devour.

> 1 Peter 5:8

No believer need ever retire. No period of life need be unfruitful. This is true even if one is wheelchair bound or bed ridden. It requires more development in spirit to pray consistently than to preach, to sing, or to organize. It is the most important thing anyone can do for God or man. One must be willing to discipline oneself to the life of prayer. This is real Christian service for any retired person. The Psalmist says it well.

> The righteous man will flourish like a palm tree, he will grow like a cedar in Lebanon; planted in the house of the LORD. They will flourish in the courts of our God. They will still yield fruit in old age. They shall be full of sap and very green, to declare, that the LORD is upright; He is my Rock, and there is no unrighteousness in Him.
>
> Psalm 92:12-15

Jesus is our rock in our older years and throughout all of life.

Notes

1   Genesis 3:24

2   *Revelation 22:2*

3   C.S. Lewis for the Third Millennium

CHAPTER 12

Our Purpose Comes From Our Creator

In the Introduction we highlighted the question JD asked in his blog post. "Is there an overarching and knowable purpose to our existence?" He further said that he didn't have a religion and didn't believe in the existence of a god. He answered his question by saying that everyone has the same purpose, that being *individual happiness*. Yet he identified the problem with his answer by stating one condition: one person's happiness must not infringe upon another's." Without the existence of God it makes his answer of individual happiness as the goal for each person untenable.

We saw further that God does desire individual happiness for all people. However, for that to exist for all people in such a way that they don't infringe on one another there must be a moral absolute that is common for all. And for there to be a single moral absolute there must be a single will of the Creator God.

Psalm 127 is called A Song of Ascent. It was one of a series of songs Jewish pilgrims sang or chanted as they climbed the path three times a year to worship at the temple in Jerusalem. It began, "Unless the Lord builds the house, they labor in vain who build it; Unless the Lord guards the city, the watchman keeps awake in vain." (Verse 1)

The joyous Psalm of thanksgiving number 100 invites us to "Shout joyfully to the Lord all the earth. Serve the Lord with gladness; Come before Him with joyful singing. Know that the Lord Himself is God; It is He who have made us and not we ourselves; We are His people and the sheep of His pasture."(vss.1-3)

We are God's creation. However, our first parents rebelled from God learning of evil along with the good. It is this rebellious nature that all mankind has inherited making it necessary for God to send The Redeemer in order to save His creation. All of this Christians confess in the three ecumenical creeds. The oldest of which is The Apostles Creed.

"I believe in God, the Father Almighty, Creator of heaven and earth, and in Jesus Christ, His only Son, our Lord, who was conceived by the Holy Spirit, born of the Virgin Mary, suffered under Pontius Pilate, was crucified, died and was buried; He descended into hell; on the third day He rose again from the dead; He ascended into heaven, and is seated at the right hand of God the Father Almighty; from there He will come to judge the living and the dead. I believe in the Holy Spirit, the Holy Christian Church, the communion of Saints, the forgiveness of sins, the resurrection of the body, and life everlasting. Amen."

A Nation Founded on a Creed

I am writing this Revised Edition of my book about midyear and particularly around the American July 4th Independence Day celebrations. I only call attention to this to highlight an observation by the British intellectual G.K.Chesterton when he visited the U.S.in 1921. *What I Saw in America* "It is a nation like no other. America, said Chesterton, is "the only nation in the world that is founded on a creed." That creed is that all men are created equal. "There is no basis for democracy except in a dogma about the divine origin of man." Thus, America is necessarily a religious nation. Chesterton says in fact, that it has "the soul of a church."

Other nations were founded on the basis of race, or by the power of kings or emperors who accumulated land and peasants who inhabited those lands. This was the difference between the American Revolution of 1776 and the French Revolution of 1789. America based their quest for "Life, Liberty, and the Pursuit of Happiness" on the equality of mankind based on their Devine creation. The French sought "Liberty, Equality, and Fraternity" based only on what the revolutionaries could accomplish. Thus the French entered a period called the Reign of Terror creating a blood bath of any perceived opposition.

Maturity Must be Nurtured and Passed On

What has all this to do with initial theme of growing in maturity as children of God? The word mature comes from the Latin *maturius* meaning to bear fruit. We know how this happens in nature and the amount of work it takes to have a fruit tree or a grape vine bear good fruit. Jesus even uses this as an illustration in St. John's gospel. Jesus said,

> I am the vine and my Father is the vine dresser. Every branch in
> Me that does not bear fruit, He takes away; and every branch
> that bears fruit, He prunes it so that it may bear more fruit.

John 15:1-2

A common definition for being mature is that "one can properly manage their behavior and respond to adverse situations acceptably or properly". Understanding maturity implies three things. Things that we have been reiterating throughout this book.

One - That there is a goal or end purpose to realize good fruit in a growing person.

Two -That there is an absolute standard by which good fruit is determined.

Three - That it takes a mature guiding hand to administer or pass on that standard.

Thus, we saw in Chapter Six that *Life Isn't Fare* in other words we all face a need to respond to adverse situations acceptably or properly. Then we examined how the various Life's Laboratory's place us in learning situations that prune us helping us to respond acceptably. That is, in ways that are helpful to others and satisfactory for ourselves. Also, the particular situation may only be one step in a longer building process.

The key, however, is that maturity needs to nurture future maturity. This is where I believe we are facing serious difficulties in today's world. Chapter Seven highlighted the Family as being a vital place where individuals mature but this also places a great burden on parents to be mature themselves so that they raise children to maturity. This unfortunately is where our modern world has failed.

An Unnurtured Generation

In the Introduction I called attention to Professor Kreeft's analysis that "We are the first civilization that does not know why we exist. Every past civilization has had some religious answer to that question. The essence of modernity is the abandoning of that religions foundation." It is always somewhat flexible to try to place a beginning date on our modern civilization, but for our purposes we can go back to the later 1940s and into the 1950. In other words this author's generation. The changes we've seen take place in the last 75 years have been phenomenal. They have made many tasks easier for the average person, but have essentially filled our time with a lot of fluff that doesn't require us to analyze and compare the real nature of the progress we made with what we believe our Lord desires as a standard for His people. It has also pulled us away from extended time with other people in a meaningful way.

I was interested in a public television program some months ago looking at the major TV personalities and variety shows of the 1950s and their major following of viewers. Zenith developed the first wireless TV remote control in 1955. It became more popular and available into the 1960s ushering in the era of "channel surfing". This was the end of the major variety shows and some of its personalities. This is a minor illustration, but I think an example of how seeming labor saving devices and modern conveniences cause vast changes in our lives.

Bring that into our era with the internet, smart phone, Google, and now Artificial Intelligence. We do thing more quickly, and more conveniently, but are they really better? Do they really support our maturing process in a God honoring way? Do they really help nurture young people to bear good fruit? I'm not advocating throwing all these aside. I'm only trying to help us think about where we are, and what really is of value for a child of God.

Are we willing to give up or deny ourselves certain things of our modern society even if we have to endure ridicule or worse?

Learning to Love others with the Love of Jesus

Maturing in a life characterized by reflecting the love of Jesus is the goal God desires for His children. It is in this maturity we find our greatest joy and happiness. We must again understand some of the terms we use. They are clearly different from the modern societal concepts. What does it mean to love someone?

Our Lord God is always our standard for truth. Probably the best definition in Scripture for love comes from St. John's gospel.

> For God so loved the world that He gave His only begotten Son that whoever believes in Him shall not perish, but have eternal life.
>
> John 3:16

The love of God is defined as doing for another all that is for their good even if it requires personal sacrifice. Love seeks to do the very best for the beloved where that best is defined by bringing that one back into harmony with their Creator God. This requires another definition, and one that our modern world rejects. We are called to separate the sin from the sinner.

Our modern culture wants us to declare that if you say you love me you will love all that I am. For a Christian these two must be separated as Jesus did. This becomes clear in John 8 when the Jewish leaders bring a woman to Jesus who was caught in the act of adultery. They wanted to trick Jesus in going against the Law of Moses which was so important to them. "The law says we are to stone such a woman. What do you say?" (vs.5) Jesus response was one of grace and truth. "He who is without sin... throw the first stone at her."(vs.7) All of the accusers slowly walked away leaving Jesus and the woman alone. No one was left to condemn her. Jesus said, "I do not condemn you either. Go. From now on sin no more."(vs.11) He did not say her actions were fine. He clearly identified adultery as sin, but separated that from the person whom he had just redeemed.

In Matthew nineteen Jesus speaks to the situation of divorce and remarriage which expands to the whole area of the proper God given sexual desires.

> Some Pharisees came to him to test him. They asked, "Is it lawful for a man to divorce his wife for any and every reason?" "Haven't you read," he replied, "that at the beginning the Creator 'made them male and female,' and said, 'For this reason a man will leave his father and mother and be united to his wife, and the two will become one flesh'? So they are no longer two, but one flesh. Therefore what God has joined together, let no one separate." "Why then," they asked, "did Moses command that a man give his wife a certificate of divorce and send her away?" Jesus replied, "Moses permitted you to divorce your wives

because your hearts were hard. But it was not this way from the beginning. I tell you that anyone who divorces his wife, except for sexual immorality, and marries another woman commits adultery." The disciples said to him, "If this is the situation between a husband and wife, it is better not to marry." Jesus replied, "Not everyone can accept this word, but only those to whom it has been given. For there are eunuchs who were born that way, and there are eunuchs who have been made eunuchs by others—and there are those who choose to live like eunuchs for the sake of the kingdom of heaven. The one who can accept this should accept it."

Matthew 19:3-12

The term eunuch here identifies a man who does not or cannot have a normal marital sexual relationship with a woman. Jesus identifies this type of man in three categories. One category was those made eunuchs by others. That is surgically as was common in royal kingdoms of Jesus day. For example, the Ethiopian Eunuch Philip encountered in Acts 8:26f. Then Jesus said there are some who choose to live like eunuchs for the sake of the kingdom of heaven. St. Paul may be considered in this category. (See 1 Corinthians 7:1-7) Jesus does defines some men as being born that way. In that case it is who they are. It is part of their nature. Even as each of us is born with certain gifts or characteristics that are a part of us. We are all called to seek the Lord for how He would have us use what we've be given for good and for His glory. However, in no case does Jesus accept the propriety of homosexual relationships or gay marriage. This was the situation in Sodom and Gomorrah which was strongly condemned. This is where the whole LGBTQ movement goes wrong.

It is not my place or desire to condemn anyone and I do not. But neither can I depart from the proper God ordained sexuality of creation.

He made them male and female in His image. To try to declare otherwise is to denigrate the very image of God.

We can only find the depth of joy and individual happiness when we are willing to seek it in the only way our Creator has designed. We will find that it is infinitely superior to any way we might try to define for ourselves. We find it by yielding to our Lord's perfect will.

Yielding

On this earth, we are called to yield to the shaping hand of our Lord. We can choose to cooperate with God by yielding to His maturing hand, or resisting Him in the lessons He brings to us in life. If we desire to be like Him, to grow into His nature, He will use all the circumstances of life to train us for His Kingdom. His desire is that we share in His nature of agape, self-sacrificing love. Life gives us the opportunities to put aside our selfishness and show His love, thus reflecting Him to others.

I try to choose words carefully. That is why I like the word yielding. I have tried to make clear that it is only God, the Holy Spirit, that can mold this life of love in us. It is not by self discipline, and screwing up our own courage to show love through gritted teeth. We can't do it ourselves. Our fallen nature fights against God's love. There is nothing in our nature that loves an enemy, or blesses those who curse us, or prays for those who mistreat us, or feeds a hungry enemy. We are to do these things so that we may be "sons of our Father who is in heaven," (Matthew 5:45) But these things simply are not in us. They will not happen unless God changes our heart. God gives us the situations in life where this response is desired. We yield to Him. That is a passive term meaning that we seek Him, cry out to Him to work this response in us. We recognize what is desired in Jesus' words, and we ask our Lord to form this in us more and more. As He does, our nature is changed and it begins to come out of us because we are being made like Him. Paul wrote, "I have been crucified with Christ; it is no longer I who live, but Christ lives in me, and the life I now live in the flesh, I live by faith in the Son of God, who loved me and gave himself up for me." (Galatians 2:20)

The Glories of the Kingdom

What God has planned for us is beyond all comprehension. Paul got a small glimpse of this when, in a vision, he was "caught up to the third heaven." (2 Corinthians 12:2) It was so wonderful that there were no words he could use afterward to speak of it. The major point here is that we do not live for this life only, but for that which God has for us after this life. We are growing toward our place in the Kingdom.

CONCLUSION

Opposition to Maturity
"Indeed, Has God Said....?"

These are the words of the Tempter in Genesis 3:1. The fallen archangel Lucifer in the form of a serpent questioned the woman about the command that God gave not to eat of the tree of the knowledge of good and evil. (Genesis 2:17) He misrepresents the original command essentially saying God has deceived them and eating from that tree will really give them a much better life. This has pitted mankind's will against God's will ever since.

We've noted previously that God created the man and woman in His own image, destining them for rulership in His eternal Kingdom. The concept of being created in God's image was declared about no other of God's created beings. Even the three great archangels, Michael, Gabriel, and Lucifer did not have this distinction. It is this image Lucifer, in his pride, wanted for himself causing him to fall from grace as he sought to "ascend above the heights of the clouds; I will make myself like the Most High."(Isaiah 14:14) It is this pride that has placed us in a spiritual battle ever since.

Lucifer, now declared the devil and Satan, cannot win. He, and the hoard of angels who fell with him, are a defeated force. To his prideful boast God said, "Nevertheless you will be thrust down to Sheol, to the recesses of the pit."(Isaiah 14:15) God has allowed him to continue for a time, even using him for our growth to maturity. We saw this with Paul's thorn in the flesh. He calls the infirmity a messenger of Satan which caused him to rely more fully upon God's grace. (2 Corinthians 12:7-10) This is where we rely upon the sure promise of our Lord that "God causes all things to work together for good to those who love God, to those who are called according to His purpose." (Romans 8:28) We have seen this prove itself out time and again in our own lives.

The Battle is Intense

We also saw how changes are coming about at a more rapid pace than we've seen before. The time of our Lord Jesus' return is only know to God, the Father, so we do not try to predict dates. But we are taught to watch, to be aware, to long for, and to pray for Christ's soon return. I call attention to this because of the daily happenings we see before us, events like no other time in history.

* A worldwide epidemic that takes a million lives and alters the lives of billions.

* A worldwide heat wave of temperatures higher than anytime in recorded history.

* Gun violence, wars, flooding, earthquakes, and famine continue to disrupt the lives of millions upon millions in various places.

* I would also call attention to man's creation of Artificial Intelligence. Proponents and detractors alike declare that this will change the lives of all mankind.

This is a Spiritual Warfare we all face. As Christians, as believers in the Lord Jesus Christ, we know the outcome of this war. We are victorious. We also know that God "is patient toward (us) not wishing for any to perish, but for all to come to repentance." (2Peter 2:9) But we must be seriously discerning about these daily happening and what they ask of us.

What Sort of People Ought You To Be?

Second Peter Chapter Three

We've said throughout that God's desire is that we understand and reflect the love of Jesus. The sacrificial love that is willing to go the second mile, and even to do good to those who spitefully use us. (Matthew 5:44) This is the image of God. The image of One who was willing to take the punishment we justly deserve into His own righteous body. "While we were yet sinners, Christ died for us." (Romans 5:8)

Evangelism is more than giving out Bibles and seeking to get someone to say the sinners prayer. These are important, but they must see the love of Jesus reflected in our lives. Only this will give them the desire to enter His sheepfold. They see that this is where they will find the best food, the best life, and the depth of peace that passes all understanding.

A New Heaven and Earth

But the day of the Lord will come like a thief, in which the heavens will pass away with a roar and the elements will be destroyed with intense heat, and the earth and its works will be destroyed. Since all these things are to be destroyed in this way, what sort of people ought you to be in holy conduct and godliness, looking for and hastening the coming of the day of God, because of which the heavens will be destroyed by burning, and the elements will melt with intense heat! But according to His promise we are looking for new heavens and a new earth, in which righteousness dwells. Therefore, beloved, since you look for these things, be diligent to be found spotless and blameless by Him, at peace, and regard the patience of our Lord as salvation; just as also our beloved brother Paul, according to the wisdom given him, wrote to you, as also in all his letters, speaking in them of these things, in which there are some things that are hard to understand, which the untaught and unstable distort, as they do also the rest of the

Scriptures, to their own destruction. You therefore, beloved, knowing this beforehand, be on your guard so that you are not carried away by the error of unscrupulous people and lose your own firm commitment, but grow in the grace and knowledge of our Lord and Savior Jesus Christ. To Him be the glory, both now and to the day of eternity. Amen.

2 Peter 3:11-18

May you ever grow in God's grace as His Holy Spirit daily walks with you.

Amen.

BIBLIOGRAPHY

Billheimer, Paul E., *Don't Waste Your Sorrows* , Fort Washington, PA, Christian Literature Crusade, 1977

Kreeft, Peter, *C. S. Lewis For The Third Millennium*, San Francisco, Ignatius Press, 1994

Hazlett, William, trans., *Luther's Table Talk*, Philadelphia, The Lutheran Publication Society.

Lewis, C. S., *Mere Christianity*, New York, N.Y. Macmillian Publishing Co. 1952

Lewis, C. S., *The Screwtape Letters*, New York, NY, Simon and Schuster, Touchstone Books, 1996

Lutheran Service Book: Pew Edition, St. Louis, Concordia Publishing House, 2006

Marnell, William H., *Man-Made Morals: Four Philosophies That Shaped America*, Garden City, New York, Anchor Books edition, Doubleday & Company, Inc., 1968

Olson, David H., Amy Olson-Sigg, & Peter Larson, *The Couple Checkup*, Nashville: Thomas Nelson, 2008

Snow, Laura Barton, *"This Thing is From Me"*, Midnight Cry Messanger, January-February 1981

Thomas, Cal, *Religious Right R.I.P.*, November , 2008, Tribune Media Service, Inc. Buffalo, N.Y.

ADDITIONAL VALUABLE RESOURCES

Jones, Peter, *One or Two, Seeing a World of Difference, Romans 1 for the Twenty-first Century*. Copyright 2010 by Main Entry Edition

Burk, Denny; et.al., *Male & Female He Crated Them, A study on Gender, Sexuality & Marriage*. Copyright 2023, Christian Focus Publications Ltd.

Breakpoint Daily, Charles Colson Center, on-line commentary @ breakpoint.org, The Colson Center, P.O. Box 62160, Colorado Springs, CO 80962,

Printed in the USA
CPSIA information can be obtained
at www.ICGtesting.com
LVHW041820240823
756139LV00005B/519